The Happiness Model

The Happiness Model

A ROADMAP TO INNER PEACE

KARTHIK GANESH

aikya

Copyright © 2018 Karthik Ganesh
All rights reserved.

No part of this book may be reproduced, or stored in a retrieval system, or transmitted in any form or by any means, electronic, mechanical, photocopying, recording, or otherwise, without express written permission of the publisher.

Published by Karthik Ganesh (Aikya Strategies), Bridgewater NJ

Edited and Designed by Girl Friday Productions
www.girlfridayproductions.com

Editorial: Irene Billings, Phyllis DeBlanche
Interior Design: Paul Barrett
Cover Design: Alban Fischer
Image Credits: Cover images © katyau/Adobe Stock; © kateja_f/iStock; © Homunkulus28/iStock

ISBN (Paperback): 9780692086872
e-ISBN: 9780692086889

First Edition

Printed in the United States of America

Dedicated to my daughter and guide, Zoey.

CONTENTS

What Is The Happiness Model? 1

PRINCIPLE 1:   Spirituality Is the Goal 15

PRINCIPLE 2:   Surrender to Everything That Happens . . . 39

PRINCIPLE 3:   Perform Actions Without Expectations
                and With Gratitude. 57

PRINCIPLE 4:   Manage Your Ego 75

PRINCIPLE 5:   Build Equanimity 85

Personalizing the Happiness Model. 99

About the Author 105

CHAPTER 1

WHAT IS *THE HAPPINESS MODEL*?

MY STORY

My daughter, Zoey, passed away from an inoperable brain tumor on November 25, 2012. She was five years old. As it is for most parents who deal with the death of a child, my wife and I were devastated. She was my life, my love, my everything, and when she passed I struggled to imagine how I could survive as well.

Looking back, I would describe myself prior to Zoey's passing as a career-obsessed, materialistic, and relatively short-tempered man, with a personal life that revolved primarily around my wife, Suman, and Zoey. Like many people, any feelings I had of emptiness or incompleteness I filled by complaining, followed by making a material acquisition. My materialistic attempts at filling the void were never really successful and were compounded by this persistent feeling about Zoey that, in hindsight, I can chalk up to intuition more than anything else. I would repeatedly tell Suman and my parents that I felt I was running out of time with her. Since she was five years old and healthy, these feelings didn't make sense to them.

Zoey had been a little sluggish for a couple of weeks and had even vomited twice for no apparent reason. We had taken her to her pediatrician, and her symptoms were chalked up to a viral infection of some kind. Our nightmare began on the morning of August 31, 2012, when Suman called me at work and told me Zoey had vomited on an empty stomach before eating her breakfast and that we needed to take her to the pediatrician. I rushed into my boss's office and told her that Zoey had a tumor and I needed to hurry home. I have no idea why those words came out of my mouth, but that was the first time in that twenty-four-hour window when I was surprised at the thoughts that were crossing my mind. At the time of Zoey's diagnosis, Suman was pregnant with our second child and was somewhat restricted in her movements. She had been on bed rest when she was pregnant with Zoey and in general needed to be extra careful when pregnant. As a result, when we took Zoey to the Children's Hospital of Philadelphia (CHOP) for an MRI on August 31, I stayed alone overnight with her in the hospital as they prepped her for the next day's scan. That night, as I was snuggled up to my daughter, I dreamed we would be told the next day that Zoey was dying from a tumor. I distinctly remember thinking to myself for the second time in twenty-four hours that I needed to stop having such negative thoughts.

The next morning, my in-laws and Suman arrived at the hospital in time for the MRI. After the procedure, the oncologist pulled Suman and me aside to let us know that Zoey had been diagnosed with Diffuse Intrinsic Pontine Glioma (DIPG)—an inoperable brain tumor with a nonexistent survival rate. Western medicine offered no options for Zoey's DIPG. We were beyond shocked. Our little girl, who had become the centerpiece of our lives, had cancer. Suman fell into uncontrollable tears, with disbelief thrown in for good measure. The only words that she kept repeating were "How is this possible? This is our Zoey." While I was crying profusely as well, my feelings were a combination of shock and guilt. Shock because cancer had always felt like something that happened to someone else, and this was my girl... How could it be possible? Why us? And I felt guilty because of my dream from earlier that morning, where Zoey's diagnosis had almost been foretold to me; in some irrational way, I felt I had caused it to happen. I came out of the oncologist's office and told my father-in-law that Zoey would not make it past the end of the year—my words, not those of her oncologist—and then proceeded to call my parents in India to let them know the same.

Throughout her "treatment," which consisted of radiation, homeopathy, and alternative Eastern remedies, there were times when she seemed more alert and ready to pull off a miracle. Strangely enough, I didn't share the miracle-related optimism of Suman and Zoey's grandparents, who were staying with us now to lend support. I remember having a conversation with my aunt, who was also with us for support, in which she asked me to have faith in God and believe that we would experience a miracle and Zoey would be healed. My response to her was that prayers were just checking a box in terms of God as a means to save Zoey, and that I felt strongly that Zoey was not going to make it. I also told her that now was the time to perform my duty as Zoey's dad, knowing that nothing I did would change the outcome.

I am not sure why such words came out of my mouth, because I would have loved to believe that Zoey would be different from every other child who had died from DIPG, but the voice in my head kept telling me otherwise. Not being able to do anything to create a different outcome was incredibly frustrating. Zoey meant everything to me, and numerous times while driving I felt like just ramming my car into a truck on the highway and ending my life. I couldn't see a life without Zoey as one worth living. Thankfully, I didn't do anything stupid and was able to be there for my daughter when she needed me the most.

Zoey was seeming to respond well to her radiation therapy when one morning she complained of a neck ache. While the folks at home thought she might have merely slept incorrectly, the same voice in my head showed up again with a different opinion. I found myself telling them that the tumor was getting more aggressive and that this was the beginning of the end. Another MRI confirmed the aggressive growth of the tumor, and she was put on palliative care within the next two days. Zoey's neck pain got progressively worse, and she couldn't comfortably lie flat on the bed. She would sit on our bed snuggled up to me for the brief moments when she was awake, and when the pain-management drugs kicked in, she would recline against me in a semi-upright position and sleep.

In one of those moments when she was awake and lucid, she waited for her mom to leave the room and then whispered that she had a secret she wanted to share with me. She proceeded to tell me that little Krishna (a Hindu god whom she fell in love with, post-diagnosis) had asked her to come and play with him, and she wanted my permission to do so. I told her to go play with him, because in his playground she would be free of the boo-boo in her head and have a lot of fun.

A week before Thanksgiving, I asked my aunt, whom Zoey loved immensely, to come back from Boston and visit Zoey, because I didn't think she would live to see December. We had been given no time frame by her oncologist, but I could tell Zoey was getting ready to say goodbye. Three days before Zoey's passing, I decided to move her back into the hospital, where her pain could be better managed. I could tell that this wasn't going to be a popular decision in the house, because I believed that everyone was still holding out for a miracle, and moving her to the hospital would be seen as a submission to defeat. Suman in particular was not OK with my decision, because she wanted to maximize Zoey's waking moments with her at home. While I was a decent dad, Suman was an incredible mother to Zoey and had quit working multiple times over the years to be able to spend time with her. Zoey and Suman were inseparable. Suman fervently believed at that time that something miraculous would happen and Zoey would survive. There were times when I wished I had the undying optimism of a mother who refused to accept that death would be the outcome. But the voice in my head still maintained that it was the right thing to do for Zoey to better manage her pain, and that Zoey had very little time left.

The night before we moved Zoey back to the hospital, I headed to the kitchen for a glass of water, feeling incredibly isolated as a result of my decision. Suman's sister, Asha, whom I had always felt was as much my little sister as she was my wife's, was staying with us to help out and be with Zoey. Zoey loved Asha immensely, and Asha in turn had always been there for every important occasion in Zoey's life, including her birth and nearly every birthday. Asha found me in the kitchen and told me to follow my instincts and know that she would always stand by my decision, because I would never do wrong by Zoey. Her words were exactly what I needed to hear, and I felt Zoey had made her stop by the kitchen to have that conversation with me.

We moved Zoey to the hospital the next morning. That was the last evening when she was completely conscious. Her last real meal was ice cream, per her request. Zoey passed away thirty-six hours later, before the end of the year, just as the voice in my head had predicted. She had survived fewer than four months from her first symptoms and fewer than three months from the time of her diagnosis.

Like many people, I always tended to overanalyze everything in life. After Zoey's passing, I thought back to the voice in my head and the constant messages of things to come that almost prepared me for the unthinkable before it happened. What had made me listen to the voice? The answer came back loud and clear: I had "surrendered" to the voice and the messages without overthinking them. Had I overanalyzed the messages from the voice, I would have become more desperate to try to save her, and the lack of medical options would have been incredibly frustrating. Instead, the voice allowed me to progress through my paternal duty without paying excessive heed to the likely outcome.

I could never call myself a religious person, and my relationship with God had always been transactional—that is, I asked God for things and prayed to God when I needed them. About a week after Zoey's passing, I went to the video store to bring home a Hindi movie because I felt it would be a distraction for all of us at home. The movie was one I didn't recognize, but it turned out to be about parents who had lost their child in an accident. The dead boy communicates with his parents through a medium, saying that he needs them to make peace with what happened and find happiness again. I saw this as a clear sign from Zoey. I experienced numerous other signs that she was around me and that I needed to trust the path she was leading me down. One of her signs resulted in my reaching out to an acquaintance who had gone through a different kind of personal grief, and, importantly, he pointed me in the direction of Brian Weiss's and Michael Newton's books on rebirth and past life regressions. That acquaintance and I are as close as brothers now.

Although I had surrendered to the voice during Zoey's illness and after her passing, the futility of life kept coming back to me. Why are we here? What is our purpose? How could there be a God if he couldn't save my little girl from dying? And why Zoey? All through this questioning, the voice and the signs kept appearing. I found that it was comforting to surrender to the voice and read the signs, even though none of my questions were being answered.

At this point, the voice in my head had morphed into Zoey's voice. One day, she nudged me toward the ancient Indian philosophy of Vedanta. Her voice told me that we were now getting to the point where my life needed to pivot and that this philosophy would help me better understand my journey and the destination. Vedanta as a philosophy predates organized religion—I call it *religion agnostic*—and it is truly timeless, since the origins of the philosophy are unknown and were passed down verbally over generations long before the organizing structure of any religion took shape. Vedanta drives home the realization that everything is God and that God is also within us.

In my viewpoint, one of the most powerful aspects of the Vedanta philosophy is the set of five principles it puts forth to help us cleanse our minds and find inner peace and happiness. At the end of the day, isn't that what we are all after? For the sake of simplicity, I'm going to refer to this five-point system as *The Happiness Model* over the course of this book. I have embraced and practiced the model over the last four years and have found tremendous personal results. *The Happiness Model* is tried and true, and it should serve as a practical guide if you are mentally stressed and looking for inner peace, have experienced a deep personal tragedy and are looking for answers, or are interested in better understanding how ancient Eastern philosophies like Vedanta lay out a real-world roadmap for happiness and fulfillment. This book is my attempt to share that model with you in the hope that you may find similar acceptance and peace.

GOD, UNIVERSE, LIFE

There are some fundamental concepts that need to be better understood prior to embracing *The Happiness Model*. The term *God* as referenced across this book is the first of them.

I use the term *God* very liberally in this context. It is important to understand that the reference to God here is not in any religious sense. I intend the word *God* to refer to the universe, a supreme power, or even simply something that's bigger than us. You are a part of this universe, as am I. It will be very difficult to embrace *The Happiness Model* discussed in this book without a strong element of faith in this larger something.

The Happiness Model is based on a realization that God is everywhere and everything is God. The notion that everything is God is a tough one to comprehend, since as humans we are more inclined to associate ourselves with concepts that we can relate to using our sense organs. With our senses being sight, touch, hearing, taste, and smell, we feel the need to connect a concept like God with one of those sense organs. Please don't misunderstand my calling God a concept here; it is, however, imperative that we understand God conceptually as the foundation of everything.

There is an order to things in this universe. Have you ever wondered where that order comes from? Day is followed by night, and then day appears again. Tides rise and fall and then rise again. The human body is considered the finest machine there is. The *circle of life*, as it is eloquently referred to in *The Lion King*, alludes to a natural progression of life and events along the food chain that take place in perfect harmony. The seasons perfectly follow each other . . . I could go on and on. The universe has been around for billions of years and has maintained that order for that duration as well. As humans, we need traffic lights and stop signs just to maintain order on the roads that we drive on. The perfect maintenance of order across the entire universe and within us as a part of that universe requires an overall method of governance. And that overall governor is also referred to in this book as God.

As you read the word *God* in my narrative, you might also want to consider God to be pure love. When we read about the prophets, avatars, and holy men and women from the years past, we come to appreciate the fact that they loved everyone and didn't distinguish between themselves and others. Concepts of family and friendship existed for these people, but not as a means to portion out love. *Love* is also the God referred to in this book.

Based on your system of faith and belief, please feel free to use the terms *God*, *universe*, and *life* interchangeably. As I mentioned earlier, faith is the bedrock of *The Happiness Model*: not faith in a religious sense, but faith in love, faith that there are no coincidences and that things happen as they are supposed to, faith in people, and faith in ourselves. All that faith is what I am calling God.

LAW OF KARMA

> *"Give, and it will be given to you. A good measure, pressed down, shaken together, running over, will be put into your lap. For with the measure you use, it will be measured back to you."*
> —Luke 6:38

> *For every action, there is an equal and opposite reaction.*
> —Newton's third law of motion

We have the feeling that if good things happen to good people, something bad could not happen to us. This feeling is accentuated when we believe that we've led perfectly good lives and have no reason to be dealt anything bad. But when something bad happens, we question God—"Why me?"—and as a result, we question our faith in God. Why would God want one person to be sad and another to be happy? Even if we don't believe that everything is God and instead believe that God is a singular creator, the hallmark of faith in God is the belief that God is impartial.

The law of karma explains everything that happens to us, whether good or bad. The law of karma simply says that every thought, intention, word, and action is governed by cause and effect. Essentially, what we think, what we say, and what we do have consequences. While the majority of the world now refers to *karma* as a noun and believes it accounts for bad things boomeranging back to bad people, that is not really an effective explanation of the law of karma at all. The law applies to good and bad thoughts, actions, and speech. For those of us who remember our basic science, the law of karma is Newtonian: every action has an equal and opposite reaction (Newton's third law of motion). In the case of karma, we interpret *every action* to include physical, mental, and verbal ones.

Lots of people think the notion of destiny is fatalistic—that whatever will happen will happen, and there's nothing we can do about it. The beauty of karma is that it single-handedly takes out any notion of fatalism. We don't control our past, because it has happened. We don't control the present that has arrived either, because it is here. We do, however, have the ability to exercise our free will and respond to the present situation in a poised manner with integrity while embracing a strong sense of right and wrong. Our current situation, or the present that has arrived, is a result of our past karma, but our reaction to the present situation drives our future karma. While we cannot control the past, if we do the right things in the present, then we accumulate good karma, which impels us toward a more pleasant future. Every thought, action, or speech results in a karmic event and a corresponding debit or credit in our account in the bank of karma. An empty account balance equates to godliness and symbolizes the ultimate state of mental and spiritual purity—that is, a state where we have no karmic debts left to pay.

Karma is the validation of the hypothesis that God is impartial, because we take the notion of God making decisions out of the equation. We get only what we deserve, based on our karma, and not what we desire. God doesn't play favorites here and give some people all the goodness and others all the badness. Have we asked ourselves why some people are born into wealthy families while others are born into abject poverty? Why are some kids born healthy while others are born with health conditions? Why are we lucky sometimes and unlucky at other times? Why do we sometimes see defeat snatched from the jaws of victory and vice versa? The karma from our past lives and that from the present lifetime influence our current situation. Our past karma and our current response influence our future. The manner in which we respond to a current situation that could be construed as adversity determines whether we have to face the situation again or can safely consider that karmic consequence to have been paid off. If we respond to the present situation appropriately—with poise, integrity, love, compassion, or a sense of duty, as pertinent—then our current action creates a credit in our karmic account balance to negate a corresponding prior debit.

It might be helpful to think of God here as a superaccountant working on an incredible supercomputer, maintaining each individual's karmic account to perfection. This extremely complex job is made even more complex by the fact that our karmic activities depend on others and theirs depend on us as well. Our interactions with one another and with the world around us have karmic consequences, and this superaccountant needs to keep impeccable track of each of those credits and debits. Essentially, what we have here is the most sophisticated accounting system imaginable, one that needs to account for a highly intricate relationship matrix for each person.

The law of karma is based on a fundamental premise that our karmic balance carries across many lifetimes. The credits and debits don't necessarily have to happen in the same lifetime. Have you ever wondered, "I've always been good, so why has this happened to me?" It may have happened to you because of something you did in a prior lifetime. The accounting system is perfect, and there is no room for glitches. How else could one explain my prior example of an innocent kid being born into a rich home versus another being born into abject poverty? Something determines the circumstances surrounding the child's birth. That something can't be God, because an impartial God wouldn't want the kid to suffer without food and clothing and live in the midst of potential sickness. That something is karma. God's role is to provide you with the anchor to hold on to when dealing with the consequences of karma.

THE HAPPINESS MODEL

Before we jump headlong into the five principles of *The Happiness Model*, I must warn you that embracing the principles is hard work. They challenge the very core of our self-centered, materialistic selves. But here's my guarantee: if you embrace all of these five principles or even some of them, you will feel markedly more at peace and experience a heightened sense of contentment in your life. The principles laid out in this model have been around for thousands of years and are core to those people who have found inner peace and fulfillment.

These are the five principles that compose *The Happiness Model*:
1. Spirituality is the goal.
2. Surrender to everything that happens.
3. Perform actions without expectations and with gratitude.
4. Manage your ego.
5. Build equanimity.

CHAPTER 2

PRINCIPLE 1: SPIRITUALITY IS THE GOAL

The first principle of *The Happiness Model* is the foundation for all the others: spirituality is the goal. When confronted with this principle, the immediate thought that may pop into your head is that spiritual growth and a focus on becoming a better person in this lifetime are somehow at odds with the brutal challenges of a world where material successes are a measure of a person's progress, leaving very little time for spirituality or any such pursuits. Another thought might be that this sounds awfully naive, since making a ton of money to live a life of comfort is, for many, the supreme goal.

It is critical to understand as we dig deeper into this principle that a heightened focus on spiritual growth doesn't mean one should become a hermit and give up materialistic desires. It also doesn't mean that we should not focus any longer on achieving our financial goals, whatever they may be. It is about understanding spirituality as our primary goal—a bigger focus than our secondary goals. When we go to a restaurant, we are clear about what the entrée is and what the sides comprise. Understanding that spiritual development is the entrée in our lives and that materialistic goals are the sides is important.

WE ARE SPIRITUAL BEINGS IN PHYSICAL BODIES

If everything that happens in our present is a result of our past karma, and everything that happens in the future is a result of our current karma (our intent and actions), then it is important, as I mentioned earlier, to appreciate that karma spans lifetimes. That tells us that there is something about us that transcends lifetimes and physical bodies. That something is the soul. The soul is a constant across lifetimes and physical bodies.

When we are an infant and turn into a little toddler and then progress onward into youth, middle age, old age, and death, at every point in that evolution we are unable to turn the clock back. At every phase of that evolution, our prior version dies and the next version is born. The same thing happens when we eventually close the curtains on this lifetime: we shed this physical body, and the next phase of our evolution arrives, where we pick another body and continue on our spiritual journey. Our soul, or the real "I," is a constant through all that change; the soul never perishes. As humans, we're generally analytical, so let's think about this analytically. As we evolve along each phase of our physical journey, we change. *Change* is a relative term and can only be validated in contrast to something static. As a person evolves, the only static construct is the real "I," or the soul. This soul is God.

Over the course of our life, we are presented with opportunities to grow spiritually. The superaccountant, God, presents these spiritual-development opportunities to us on the basis of our past karma and in the hope that we handle them appropriately, with the right attitude, intentions, and actions. The adage we hear about how "God never gives you more than you can handle" is very appropriate. My broader point, though, is that spiritual development comes from dealing with life's challenges without labeling them "good" or "bad" and from handling them with poise and grace. We naturally grow up in an environment where everything is labeled as "good" or "bad" based on our perspective. The important message here is that this label is exactly that: a perspective. When it rains outside just as we are making plans to head out, we curse the weather and label it "bad." On the other hand, that very same rain is "good" to someone in a drought-stricken area. In truth, the rain isn't "good" or "bad"; it's our perspective that gives it a label. Spiritual development is when you stop yourself just short of the point of giving it a label and just tell yourself that irrespective of the situation, it is a blessing. Poise and grace are also attributes of God.

In each lifetime, we pick up our spiritual journey where we left off in the prior lifetime, just as we pick up our karmic balance at the bank of karma. It is our responsibility and goal as spiritual beings to move the ball forward in each lifetime and evolve. The great industrialist Henry Ford had some pertinent things to say about rebirth and the continuation of our journey in the next lifetime:

> *I adopted the theory of Reincarnation when I was twenty-six. Religion offered nothing to the point. Even work could not give me complete satisfaction. Work is futile if we cannot utilize the experience we collect in one life in the next. When I discovered Reincarnation, it was as if I had found a universal plan. I realized that there was*

a chance to work out my ideas. Time was no longer limited. I was no longer a slave to the hands of the clock.[1]

It is unclear if Henry Ford was a student of Vedanta, but his view on reincarnation is now shared by a majority of people globally across a broad spectrum of religions.

TRAITS ASSOCIATED WITH SPIRITUAL DEVELOPMENT

Spiritual growth in its simplest form is an effort to become a better person in the karmic sense. Please continue to keep in mind that karma is not only about our actions, but our intentions and thoughts as well. Spiritual growth is the result of constant refinement and purification of our activities, both mental and physical. Traits that showcase spiritual growth include

- compassion toward others, especially those in need;
- empathy;
- kindness;
- being charitable (not only about money—being charitable with your time is in some cases more important than money);
- respect for other people;
- respect for the world around us, including animals and nature;
- understanding that each person has their own personal challenges and we shouldn't rush to pass judgment on others; and
- handling the dualities of life (birth-death, wealth-poverty, victory-defeat, etc.) with poise and grace.

---

1. *San Francisco Examiner*, August 26, 1928.

Here is an old Indian parable to showcase the single-minded focus of a boy on his spiritual goal. He sees everything that he encounters in life as his teacher.

Dattatreya's Single-Mindedness

One day, when Dattatreya was still a child, the king of a neighboring country came to visit the ashram (hermitage or monastic community) where the boy lived with his parents. Because his parents were away, the boy greeted the guest. As Dattatreya made arrangements for the visitor's comfort, the king saw an inner joy radiating from the boy's countenance. Realizing that this was a spontaneous expression of the intrinsic beauty of the boy's soul, he was sure that Dattatreya was gifted with great wisdom. Curious to learn how someone so young could be so wise, the king questioned the child, and the following dialogue ensued.

King: You have been studying with your parents?
Dattatreya: There is much to learn from everyone
   and everything, not only from my parents.
King: Then you have a teacher? Who is it?
Dattatreya: I have twenty-four gurus.
King: Twenty-four gurus at such a tender age? Who
   are they?
Dattatreya: Mother Earth is my first guru. She taught
   me to hold lovingly in my heart all those who
   trample me, scratch me, and hurt me, just as
   she does. She taught me to give them my best,
   remembering that their acts are normal and natural from their standpoint.
King: Who is your second guru?

Dattatreya: Water. This force contains life and purity. It cleanses whatever it touches and provides life to whoever drinks it. Water flows unceasingly. If it stops, it becomes stagnant. "Keep moving, keep moving" is the lesson I learned from water.

King: Your third guru?

Dattatreya: Fire. It burns everything, transforming it into flames. By consuming dead logs, it produces warmth and light. Thus, I learned to absorb everything that life brings and turn it into the flame that enlightens my life. In that light, others can walk safely.

King: Who is your fourth guru, sir?

Dattatreya: The wind is my fourth guru. The wind moves unceasingly, touching flowers and thorns alike, but it never attaches itself to the objects it touches. Like the wind, I learned not to prefer flowers over thorns or friends over foes. Like the wind, my goal is to provide freshness to all without becoming attached.

King: The fifth guru, sir?

Dattatreya: All-pervading and all-embracing space is my fifth guru. Space has room for the sun, moon, and stars, and yet it remains untouched and unconfined. I, too, must have room for all the diversities of existence and still remain unaffected by what I contain. All visible and invisible objects have their rightful place within me, but they have no power to confine my consciousness.

King: Who is your sixth guru, sir?

Dattatreya: The moon. The moon waxes and wanes, and yet it never loses its essence, totality, or shape. From watching the moon, I learned that waxing and waning, rising and falling, pleasure and pain, and loss and gain are simply phases of life. While passing through these phases, I never lose awareness of my true self.

King: Who is your seventh guru?

Dattatreya: The sun is my seventh guru. With its bright rays, the sun draws water from everything, transforms it into clouds, and then distributes it without favor as rain. Rain falls on forests, mountains, valleys, deserts, oceans, and cities. Like the sun, I learned how to gather knowledge from all sources, transform that knowledge into practical wisdom, and share it with all, without preferring some recipients and excluding others.

King: And your eighth guru?

Dattatreya: My eighth guru is a flock of pigeons. When one fell into a hunter's net and cried in despair, the other pigeons tried to rescue it and got caught, too. From these pigeons, I learned that even a positive reaction, if it springs from attachment and emotion, can entangle and ensnare.

King: Your ninth guru, sir?

Dattatreya: My ninth guru is the python, which catches and eats its prey, then doesn't hunt again for a long time. It taught me that once my need has been met, I must be satisfied and not make myself miserable running after the objects of my desire.

King: Who is your tenth guru?

Dattatreya: The ocean, which is the abode of the waters. It receives and assimilates water from all the rivers in the world, and yet it never overflows its boundaries. The ocean taught me that no matter what experiences I go through in life, no matter how many kicks and blows I receive, I must maintain my discipline.

King: Who is your eleventh guru, O wise one?

Dattatreya: The moth is my eleventh guru. Drawn by light, it flies from its dwelling to sacrifice itself in the flame. It taught me that once I see the dawn, I must overcome my fear, soar at full speed, and plunge into the flame of knowledge to be consumed and transformed.

King: The twelfth?

Dattatreya: My twelfth guru is the bumblebee, which takes only the tiniest drops of nectar from the flowers. And before accepting even that much, it hums and hovers and dances, creating an atmosphere of joy around the blossom. It not only sings the song of cheerfulness; it also gives more to the flowers than it takes: it pollinates the plants and helps them prosper by flying from one to another. I learned from the bumblebee that I should take only a little from nature and that I should do so cheerfully, enriching the source from which I receive sustenance.

King: Your thirteenth guru?

Dattatreya: My thirteenth guru is the honeybee, which collects more nectar than it needs. It gathers nectar from different sources, transforms it into honey, and brings it to the hive. It consumes only a bit of what it gathers and shares the rest with others. Thus, I should gather wisdom from the teachers of all disciplines and process the knowledge that I gain. I must apply the knowledge that is conducive to my own growth, but I must also be ready to share everything I know with others.

King: The fourteenth guru, O wise seeker?
Dattatreya: Once I saw a wild elephant being trapped. A tame female elephant in season was the bait. Sensing her presence, the wild male emerged from its domain and fell into a pit that had been cleverly concealed with branches and heaps of leaves. Once caught, the wild elephant was tamed to be used by others. This elephant is my fourteenth guru, because he taught me to be careful with my passions and desires. Worldly charms arouse our sensory impulses, and while chasing after these sense-based cravings, the mind gets trapped and enslaved, even though it is powerful.

King: Who is your fifteenth guru, sir?
Dattatreya: The deer, with its keen sense of hearing. It listens intently and is wary of all noises—but it is lured to its doom by the melody of the deer hunter's flute. Like the deer, we keep our ears alert for every bit of news, rumor, and gossip, and are skeptical about much that we hear. What I learned from the deer is that we become spellbound by certain words that—due to our desires, attachments, and cravings—we delight to hear. This tendency creates misery for ourselves and others.

King: And who is your sixteenth guru?
Dattatreya: The fish that swallows a baited hook and is caught by the fisherman. This world is like bait. As long as I remember the fish, I remain free of the hook.

King: Who is your seventeenth guru?
Dattatreya: A prostitute. She knows that she doesn't love her customers, and nor do they love her. She waits for them, and when they come she enacts

the drama of love, but she isn't satisfied with the artificial love she gives and receives, nor with the payment she is given. Through her I realized that all humans are like prostitutes, and the world, like the customers, is enjoying us. The payment is always inadequate, and we feel dissatisfied. Thus, I determined not to live like a prostitute. Instead, I will live with dignity and self-respect. I will not expect this world to give me either material or internal satisfaction. I will find satisfaction myself by going within.

King: Who is your eighteenth guru?

Dattatreya: My eighteenth guru is the little bird that was flying with a worm in its beak. Larger birds flew after him and began to peck him. They stopped only when the little bird dropped the worm. Thus, I learned that the secret of survival lies in renunciation, not in possession.

King: Who is your nineteenth guru, sir?

Dattatreya: My nineteenth guru is the baby who cries when it is hungry and stops when it suckles at its mother's breast. When the baby is full, it stops feeding, and nothing its mother does can induce it to take more milk. I learned from this baby to demand only what I really need. When it is provided, I must take only what I require and then turn my face away.

King: And your twentieth guru?

Dattatreya: A young woman whom I met when I was begging for alms. She told me to wait while she prepared a meal. Her bracelets jangled as she cooked, so she removed one. But the noise continued, so she took them all off one by one until only one remained. Then there was silence. Thus,

I learned that wherever there is a crowd, there is noise, disagreement, and dissension. Peace can be expected only in solitude.

King: And your twenty-first guru?

Dattatreya: A snake that makes no hole for itself, but rests in holes other creatures have abandoned, or curls up in the hollow of a tree for a while, and then moves on. From this snake, I learned to adjust myself to my environment and enjoy the resources of nature without encumbering myself with a permanent home. Creatures in nature move constantly, continually abandoning their previous dwellings. Therefore, while floating along the current of nature, I find plenty of places to rest. Once I am rested, I move on.

King: And your twenty-second guru?

Dattatreya: My twenty-second guru is the arrow maker who was so absorbed in shaping his arrowheads that the king and his entire army passed nearby without attracting his attention. Thus, I learned to be absorbed in the task at hand, no matter how big or small. The more one-pointed my focus, the greater my absorption, and the greater my absorption, the subtler my awareness. The goal is subtle; it can be grasped only by subtle awareness.

King: Your twenty-third guru?

Dattatreya: My twenty-third guru is the little spider that built itself a nice, cozy web. When a larger spider chased it, it rushed to take refuge in its web. But it ran so fast that it got entangled and was swallowed by the bigger spider. Thus, I learned that we create webs for ourselves by trying to build a safe haven, and as we race along the threads of these webs, we become entangled and are consumed. There is no safety to be found in the complicated webs of our actions.

King: And who is your twenty-fourth guru?

Dattatreya: My twenty-fourth guru is the worm that was caught by a songbird and placed in its nest. As the bird began to sing, the worm became so absorbed in the song that it lost all awareness of its peril. Watching this little creature become absorbed in a song in the face of death reminded me that I, too, must develop the art of listening so that I may become absorbed in the eternal sound that is always within me.

Listening to Dattatreya, the king realized that the wisdom of this young boy flowed from his determination to keep the goal of life firmly fixed in his awareness as well as from his ability to discover the lessons of life everywhere he turned.

SENSE OF SECURITY

We nearly always incorrectly equate financial resources, material objects, and relationships with a sense of security. Haven't we heard ourselves or others say, "Once I make my first million, I will be secure and won't ask for anything else," or "Once I have a child, I will feel complete and then won't need anything else"? We absolutely must have that job, car, piece of jewelry, home with the white picket fence, or whatever we imagine will complete us, and then, we believe, we will feel entirely secure.

When we think of financial security as an anchor, we are setting ourselves up to be disappointed. The more wealth we have, the more insecure we are about protecting it. The richer you are, the more eager you become to keep generating more wealth and the greater your fear becomes of losing it all. You came into this world empty-handed and will leave the exact same way. If all material possessions along the way are temporary, why would we let them impact our sense of security and mental well-being?

Even with our family members, we feel our spouse or child gives us a sense of security. Yet the relationship with the spouse can end in divorce, and, as happened in my case, the child can die. A person can lose millions faster than they were earned. What that tells us is that essentially everything around us is impermanent by nature. So now taking a step back and thinking about this analytically, why would we expect that holding on to things that are fundamentally unstable would give us stability? Change is the law of the universe. When everything around us is changing all the time, what can we hold on to that would actually give us a sense of stability and security? What can we truly rely on that is unchangeable, permanent, and secure? The only thing that is a constant while everything is changing around you is found within you. We will also refer to that constant anchor within you as God.

For a lot of us, the ultimate loss of security comes when a loved one dies or when we try confronting our own mortality. When Zoey passed away, my wife and I were shattered and couldn't fathom living without her. What is it about death that we fear? Is it the fear of the unknown? Is it the feeling of finitude that one associates with death? Or as it pertains to our mortality, is it as simple as not wanting to leave our loved ones behind? Maybe it's all of the above. Let's take a more dispassionate approach to death and dying and then revisit why we would tie our sense of security to life and sense of insecurity to death.

It is a scientific fact that nearly all the cells in our body die every seven years and are refreshed. In other words, we could say that we (including our loved ones) die and are reborn every seven years. As our children grow from infants to toddlers and then to little boys or girls, each phase of their life dies along the way. While parents of a teenager might tell themselves repeatedly that they would love to see their child once again be a toddler who listens to them, they realize it is impossible. Their child's toddler phase had to die for them to have a teenager now.

Discounting the act of committing suicide, death is a choiceless situation. Once we accept death to be a choiceless situation, an intelligent, analytical human mind won't be afraid of it, because death will happen when it will happen, and worrying about it won't change a thing. The cycle of creation, maintenance, destruction, and creation again is seen in nature all the time. Dawn (creation) turns into the day (maintenance), which turns into night (destruction), which then turns into dawn again the next morning. Barring suicide, which is the act of causing death in an untimely fashion, our death is always perfectly timed, because death only arrives at the culmination of this lifetime's karmic journey. Vedanta repeatedly stresses that there is never a wrong time for anything, including death. Our natural tendency when a loved one passes is to grieve, which is due to a feeling of loss. After we get past the initial feeling of loss, we should actually celebrate the person's death, because the death signifies the natural end of the trials and tribulations of this lifetime and the soul's readiness for the next.

I realize this is a counterintuitive perspective in the West, but even here there are a number of people who vocalize the need to celebrate their deceased loved ones' lives. Looking back at Zoey, I could either choose to be sad about her death or feel incredibly blessed for the life she led and shared with me. Her death, while untimely from an external viewpoint, was perfectly timed as it pertained to her soul. She had taken on this life for only five and a half years and passed away exactly when she was supposed to. When she passed, she left behind the boo-boo in her head and any other challenges or insecurities she might have had.

Have you ever seen the look of peace on a person's face after his or her death? So, if death is always perfectly timed, if we can do nothing about it, and if it results in the person going "home," why would we let it create a sense of insecurity in us? The seventeenth-century English poet Abraham Cowley famously said, "Life is an incurable disease." Understanding life and death to be two sides of the same coin and not letting fear of our own death or that of a loved one bring us down are also parts of our spiritual growth. The more appropriate way to put this would be that acceptance is an important trait of spiritual growth.

The only constant, the only anchor to depend on that is permanent and not fraught with insecurities and change, is the "I" within you. The "I" in this case is not your physical body and in fact has very little to do with it, for your physical body is dispensable as well. The "I" in this case is the strength within, the soul, also known as God. The only constant in our lives that is permanent and we can hold on to when all else changes around us is God. Everything else, every relationship, every material possession, is impermanent. Understanding that God is our secure anchor and having faith in ourselves—that is, God—to hold on to are signs of spiritual development.

You may have noticed that I haven't said anything at all about your preferred place of worship as an answer to your insecurity. That's because, like everything around you, your place of worship is also impermanent. Be it a church, temple, mosque, or synagogue, there are too many variables that make it an impermanent factor in your life: you may relocate, for example, or the structure might be shut down. The bottom line is there is nothing on the outside that is permanent to you. Your only security and anchor are within.

COMPASSION AND CHARITY

Whenever I think of compassion and charity as highly visible markers for spiritual development, my mind immediately goes to Bill Gates. I'm sure there are multiple schools of thought about him as a businessman and what Microsoft is or isn't, but I'm referring to Bill Gates as a human. Here's a synopsis of the Bill & Melinda Gates Foundation's achievements:

- Created a $43.5 billion trust committed to the eradication of malaria and polio and to controlling the spread of tuberculosis and HIV
- Led the charge to eradicate polio across the world; as of 2017, only Pakistan and Afghanistan have any reported cases
- Mortality from malaria has dropped by more than 42 percent since the foundation aggressively went after the disease

There are numerous other achievements of the foundation that could fill pages, but here's the broader point: Bill Gates was blessed to have made a significant fortune in this lifetime via a company he built himself. He has channeled that fortune toward improving the world. When Bill Gates talks about his desire to cure malaria and polio, you can hear the passion in his voice and the fervent desire to not have to see another child suffer from these diseases. He has now decided that he wants to go after Alzheimer's disease. A cynic might say that it's easy for the richest man in the world to give away his money, but cynicism is an impediment to spiritual development. Imagine how spiritually developed Bill Gates is, and aspire to showcase the same commitment to charity and compassion in your life, in whatever ways you are able. The change here is attitudinal and has nothing to do with our financial means.

ELIMINATE ANY SENSE OF ENTITLEMENT

Entitlement and expectations are the two worst enemies of happiness. Entitlement results in a buildup of expectations, which if not met results in unhappiness. Say we have a great job interview and expect to get the job, or we put a ton of effort into a project at work and expect to get promoted. In the first instance, if we don't get the job, we are dejected. In the latter, again, if we don't get the promotion, we are disappointed. We spend too much of our lives feeling entitled and then, when what we expect doesn't happen, we spend an equal amount of time being unhappy. Why would we do that to ourselves? Our problem is that we expect or feel entitled to a certain outcome, and when it doesn't happen, we automatically tag it as being the "wrong" outcome. Consider what Richard Bach, an English RAF pilot turned philosopher who penned the much-acclaimed book *Jonathan Livingston Seagull*, once wrote: "What the caterpillar calls the end of the world, the master calls a butterfly."[2] We may look at a certain outcome and be dejected by it, but it could be the exact outcome that was needed at that time. What if that job was just the wrong one for us? What if that promotion could have brought on exposure to additional office politics and eventually resulted in our termination? Here's a key message to understand: **We are only**

---

2. Richard Bach, *Illusions: The Adventures of a Reluctant Messiah* (New York: Random House, 1989).

entitled to the effort that we put in and are in no way entitled to the desired outcome.

When we perform a set of actions, let's enjoy the actions instead of brooding over the expected outcome we associate with them. The journey is more important than the destination. Vedanta talks about the fact that we are only entitled to performing our actions with the right intent and in the best possible manner; we are not entitled to the outcome we desire. "We only get what we deserve and not what we desire" is a fundamental truth that is core to the Vedanta philosophy. Once we embrace the notions that we are not going to label the outcome as "good," "bad," right," or "wrong" and that whatever the outcome is, it is the appropriate one, we find ourselves shedding our sense of entitlement and tempering our expectations, and we are not disappointed with the outcome, whatever it may be.

The same is the case with our prayers to God. In a purely nonreligious sense, it is important that we stop having a transactional relationship with God. A transactional relationship with God is one where we pray and ask for something, which I'm sure you agree is more the norm than the exception. Think about it: Don't many of us see the act of praying as being incomplete without a materialistic ask of God? When Zoey was diagnosed with a tumor, all our prayers were directed toward her being cured. We prayed for a miracle, and we got one, just not the kind we desired. Most kids who die from DIPG, which is a tumor in the brain stem, experience a gradual shutdown of the basic automatic functions controlled by the brain stem, like swallowing, breathing, and reflex control. Our miracle was that the tumor grew so fast, she passed away before it impacted these automatic functions. Her last meal being her favorite food, ice cream, was also a miracle in itself.

A transactional conversation with God will result in expectations and set you up for potential disappointment, with the end result being a questioning of God and your faith. Would it be terribly wrong for us to take the time to instead thank God for everything we've been given? Coming back to the situation with Zoey, it would have been more appropriate to thank God for the blessing of giving us a daughter like Zoey while also asking God to give us the strength to deal with the outcome gracefully. Since I stopped asking God for things of the material world (asking for good health is a materialistic ask as well), I've increased my ability to appreciate whatever comes my way. Interestingly enough, the absence of both transactional asks of God and the expectations that God will fulfill them has enormously strengthened my faith. I now believe that whatever happens is for a reason, and God always takes care of me, one way or another.

SPIRITUAL INTELLIGENCE AND LEADERSHIP

The term *spiritual intelligence* has been around for a while, but its correlation with motivational leadership hasn't been exhaustively researched. Spiritually intelligent people demonstrate greater self-awareness and poise, while constantly showcasing the importance of equanimity, self-reflection, and values in the way they communicate. With Principle 1 being focused on spirituality as the goal, I felt it important to share with you some messages I've read over the years from people I believe were highly spiritually intelligent.

Abraham Lincoln's Letter to Son's Teacher

In this letter, some say to be from Abraham Lincoln to his son's teacher, he asks her to assist in his son's spiritual development. Please note how he bids the teacher to equip his son to deal with the dualities of life in a poised manner, while also developing a spiritual and well-balanced value system.

My son starts school today. It is all going to be strange and new to him for a while and I wish you would treat him gently. It is an adventure that might take him across continents. All adventures that probably include wars, tragedy and sorrow. To live this life will require faith, love and courage.

So, dear Teacher, will you please take him by his hand and teach him things he will have to know, teaching him—but gently, if you can. Teach him that for every enemy, there is a friend. He will have to know that all men are not just, that all men are not true. But teach him also that for every scoundrel there is a hero, that for every crooked politician, there is a dedicated leader.

Teach him if you can that 10 cents earned is of far more value than a dollar found. In school, Teacher, it is far more honorable to fail than to cheat. Teach him to learn how to gracefully lose, and enjoy winning when he does win.

Teach him to be gentle with people, tough with tough people. Steer him away from envy if you can and teach him the secret of quiet laughter. Teach him if you can—how to laugh when he is sad, teach him there is no shame in tears. Teach him there can be glory in failure and despair in success. Teach him to scoff at cynics.

Teach him if you can the wonders of books, but also give time to ponder the extreme mystery of birds in the sky, bees in the sun and flowers on a green hill. Teach him to have faith in his own ideas, even if everyone tells him they are wrong.

Try to give my son the strength not to follow the crowd when everyone else is doing it. Teach him to listen to everyone, but teach him also to filter all that he hears on a screen of truth and take only the good that comes through.

Teach him to sell his talents and brains to the highest bidder but never to put a price tag on his heart and soul. Let him have the courage to be impatient, let him have the patience to be brave. Teach him to have sublime faith in himself, because then he will always have sublime faith in mankind, in God.

This is the order, Teacher, but see what best you can do. He is such a nice little boy and he is my son.

Nelson Mandela's Letter to His Wife, Winnie Mandela

In Nelson Mandela's letter to his wife below, he stresses the importance of leading a spiritual life and offers examples of spiritual values. Clearly Mandela gauged personal growth and development in spiritual and not materialistic terms.

In judging our progress as individuals, we tend to concentrate on external factors such as one's social position, influence and popularity, wealth and standard of education.

He continues:

Internal factors may be even more crucial in assessing one's development as a human being. Honesty, sincerity, simplicity, humility, pure generosity, absence of vanity, readiness to serve others—qualities which are within easy reach of every soul—are the foundation of one's spiritual life.[3]

He ends the letter with the following: "Never forget that a saint is a sinner who keeps on trying."

SPIRITUAL DEVELOPMENT AND HAPPINESS

You may have noticed that I use the terms *happiness* and *inner peace* interchangeably to a large extent. I've struggled to define *happiness* in my personal life any other way. The loss of a child is a deeply personal event, and the notion of "time heals all wounds" does not apply. The pain doesn't go away; you just learn to live with it. Yet I would say that I am not sad. I'm at peace with myself and my surroundings, including the world around me and the people I interact with. Having that level of inner peace without an element of sadness is what I'm calling happiness.

Inner peace needs work, as you can see in Principle 1 and will see in the principles that follow. Your spiritual journey is an inward one. It is a journey where progress is determined by the distance traveled within and not without. When you start making progress on that journey and find yourself becoming spiritually stronger, it will naturally give you a greater degree of inner fortitude and lead to a higher sense of inner peace—that is, happiness.

---

3. Nelson Mandela quoted in Donald McCown, Diane Reibel, and Marc S. Micozzi, *Resources for Teaching Mindfulness: An International Handbook* (Ann Arbor, MI: Springer International Publishing, 2016).

When we have empathy and compassion toward our fellow living beings, respect nature, treat others with respect, are poised in challenging situations, and keep our focus on the God within us, we naturally begin to experience a sense of calm. This sense of calm is based on an attitudinal correction toward ourselves and all things and situations around us. This sense of calm eliminates worry and helps us cleanse our minds. A clean mind divorced of worry is a happy one.

In all candor, I have somewhat struggled with the notion that not being sad equates to being happy. Happiness and sadness are also part of life's dualities. The perspective that I've landed upon after a lot of reflection is this: we need a word to define a sense of inner peace, a feeling of mental fullness (or rather one where you don't feel empty or as if you're lacking something), a high level of comfort with yourself, and the comfort in knowing that everything happens for a reason. I'm calling *happiness* that word.

Spiritual development is a journey and needs to be embraced as such. When you're on this journey and are focused on moving forward, you will notice the differences. You will be less irritable. Faced with situations that in the past would have made you angry, you will now deem them as not important enough to warrant anger. You will find yourself more accepting of the world and people around you, and in the cases where you don't like what you see, you will focus on changing your attitude toward them rather than trying to change what you don't like. You will naturally gravitate toward reading material that has depth to it and can potentially give you more tools for inner strength. You will find greater patience in your interpersonal interactions and will reduce your desire to judge others. Compassion toward others will come more easily to you.

None of this is going to happen overnight; hence I can't overstress the "journey" nature of this process. But there is no better time to begin that journey than right now. Be patient as you move forward, and if you find yourself getting derailed, gently coax yourself back in the right direction. The beauty of this entire experience is that it is completely self-contained and you have no dependencies. No one else can hamper or derail this experience. Nothing could be more deeply personal than your own spiritual development and your quest for inner peace, a.k.a. happiness.

CHAPTER 3

PRINCIPLE 2: SURRENDER TO EVERYTHING THAT HAPPENS

In the first principle, we discussed how an important part of our spiritual development is to stop assigning an attribute of "good" or "bad" to things that happen around and to us. The notion of an event or an experience being "good" or "bad" is a matter of perspective, and when we change our perspective, the binary nature of the attribute changes as well. The change in our perspective is purely an attitudinal one, and we have complete control over it.

In Principle 2, we discuss the attitude of surrendering, where we accept whatever comes our way as a blessing and keep moving forward. This is an incredibly important principle that teaches us the importance of acceptance as we progress toward the goals of equanimity and inner peace.

Surrender is an extremely intuitive and practical attitude and yet a very hard one to master. Its basis is in the core construct of faith and the belief that whatever happens, happens for a reason. Once you master it, though, unhappiness and dejection are not emotions you will need to worry about. Take everything that happens as a blessing from God. Don't give it an attribute of "good" or "bad"; just accept it to be the right thing for you and embrace the situation for what it is—a gift.

I keep coming back to the example of the weather, because in many discussions it is either a conversation starter or an enabler. It is the epitome of irrelevant small talk. How many times have we found ourselves complaining to someone about the weather? "This snow stinks," or "I hate the rain," or "Today is a really hot day, and I just can't stand the sun." In one part of the world, you have a person living in extreme heat near a desert, thinking that nothing could be better than snow. A rice farmer in India wakes up each day praying for rain. Folks in Alaska would love to see more sun. The point here is that the problem isn't the weather. The problem is our attitude toward the weather. The next time you feel like complaining about something, take a step back, accept it, and tell yourself a quiet "Thank you"; you will immediately feel a sense of calm. A sense of calm is the ultimate driver of inner peace.

The same attitudinal correction is as important to apply to things that happen to us directly as indirectly. Our lives are filled with constant dualities: profit and loss, victory and defeat, happiness and sadness, birth and death. Surrender to these dualities of life by not letting either one or the other get you too high or too low. Accept them for what they are—events that are fundamentally temporary in nature and could reverse in a heartbeat.

As I've looked back on Zoey's passing, I've decided to feel extremely blessed for the five and a half years that I had with my girl, rather than angry at the cancer that took her away. What is the point of focusing on the cancer? All it will do is make me feel negative and angry, which will result in significant unhappiness in my personal life. It would also naturally make me a very difficult person to be around, which would create unhappiness in the people around me. Why would I do this? Why would I take the perfect opportunity for spiritual development that God has given me and reject it? The key here is attitudinal as well. We must accept every single situation that we encounter with the right attitude and surrender to the notion that if it's happening to us, there must be a good reason for it. We may not necessarily be able to rationalize the reason, but we need to accept it for what it is.

This is a good opportunity for us to revisit the law of karma. There are a number of important aspects from that law that we need to consider here. Firstly, our karma and the associated balance in the bank of karma trail us across lifetimes. When something happens to us in this lifetime that we consider "bad" or suboptimal, our immediate thought might be that we've always been good to others or devout in our religious beliefs, and as a result, we are entitled to good things happening to us. What we forget is that events or experiences in this lifetime may be effects caused by actions from a past life. We have control only over how we respond to the event at the present moment. If we respond to it with the right attitude and embrace it gracefully, we will neutralize that karmic event and not need to relive it in this or another lifetime.

On the other hand, if we are unable to deal with the event gracefully, we might need to go through it again and again until we get the response right. The idea of spiritual development over many lifetimes is that we develop the ability to handle all our karmic consequences, as reflected in the dualities in life, with poise and grace. According to Vedanta, when we are able to handle all things that come our way with the right attitude because we know them to be nothing more than the closure of our karmic consequences, we are well on our way to godliness

THE HAPPINESS MODEL

or a state where our bank of karma account value is zero. The most effective way to deal with any event is to surrender to it and say a quiet "Thank you" to God for giving us the opportunity to experience it.

The loss of a child is excruciatingly tough. While Zoey's passing was and continues to be extremely hard, there are two very clear messages that I choose to take away from this experience. The first one is that dealing with the loss of a child is an experience that I may not have desired but that I deserved. This was something that, because of some past event, in some other life, I needed to go through. As I've embraced, internalized, and surrendered to that understanding, it has made all my questions of "Why did this happen to me?" go away. The second message that I have taken away is that after her passing, I clearly had multiple paths that I could have taken to deal with the pain.

Alcohol and drugs, resulting in a broken marriage and a life of feeling sorry for myself, could have been one path. Being constantly angry with God and the world around me and feeling negative all the time would have been another path. Surrendering to this experience and ensuring it made me stronger mentally and spiritually while I delivered on my responsibilities to my family was another. Zoey guided me toward the path that was appropriate for my spiritual development, and I trust her completely. Vedanta tells me this is the right path as well and that there is no greater attitude in this world than surrender based on the faith that everything happens for a reason. While I'm not sure how I will be judged in the karmic sense, I know for a fact that the path I've chosen has given me tremendous inner peace and comfort. If heaven and hell are states of mind, the alternate paths would have been hell, and the one I've chosen is heaven.

When Suman was pregnant with our first son, Anay, Zoey would see her mom's pregnant stomach and call her little brother "soccer ball." Anay was born the same month that Zoey passed away. Immediately after Zoey's passing, I struggled with the unfairness of God, who gave us a child while taking another one away. But as I started surrendering and cuddling Zoey's "soccer ball," I began to appreciate Anay's birth for what it was—God's way of throwing us a lifeline and taking care of us. While he will never remember being with her, we feel extremely blessed that he got to meet her prior to her passing. Feeding him and catering to his every need was an important distraction for Suman, ensuring she was mentally and physically busy. There is no greater way to realize God's support than to surrender. We tend to overanalyze situations, and that's where the problem lies. Here's a parable that describes this scenario to perfection.

The Man and the Flood

A terrible storm came into a town, and local officials sent out an emergency warning that the riverbanks would soon overflow and flood the nearby homes. They ordered everyone in the town to evacuate immediately. A faithful man heard the warning and decided to stay, saying to himself, "I will trust God, and if I am in danger, then God will send a miracle to save me."

The neighbors came by his house and said to him, "We're leaving, and there is room for you in our car; please come with us!" But the man declined, saying he had faith that God would save him.

As the man stood on his porch watching the water rise up the steps, a man in a canoe paddled by and called to him, "Hurry and come into my canoe; the waters are rising quickly!" But the man declined again, reconfirming his belief that God would save him.

The floodwaters rose higher, pouring water into his living room, and the man had to retreat to the second floor. A police motorboat came by and saw him at the window and shouted, "We will come up and rescue you!" But the man declined their offer of help and asked them to spend their time saving someone else, because God would save him.

The floodwaters rose higher and higher, and the man had to climb up to his rooftop. A helicopter spotted him and dropped a rope ladder. A rescue officer came down the ladder and pleaded with the man, "Grab my hand, and I will pull you up!"

But the man still refused the offer of help, folding his arms tightly to his body.

Shortly after, the house broke up and the floodwaters swept the man away, and he drowned. When in heaven, the man stood before God and asked, "I put all of my faith in you. Why didn't you come and save me?" And God said, "Son, I sent you a warning. I sent you a car. I sent you a canoe. I sent you a motorboat. I sent you a helicopter. What more were you looking for?"[4]

EMBRACE THE LACK OF CONTROL

A major inhibiting factor in our ability to surrender is our desire to be in control, or at least feel like we're in control, of

---

4. As quoted in Darlyne G. Nemeth and Traci W. Olivier, *Innovative Approaches to Individual and Community Resilience: From Theory to Practice* (London: Elsevier, 2017), and elsewhere.

situations and experiences that come our way. This applies to us both personally and professionally. An important surrender-related attitudinal change is to embrace the lack of control and accept that while we can provide the best inputs into a situation, we can't control the outcome.

Let's say you have worked really hard to secure a particular job interview, and you feel strongly that this is your dream job. You have mentally rehearsed every single question they could ask, as well as your polished answers. Maybe you've even leveraged a friend or mentor to put you through mock interviews for practice. You've already mentally drafted a letter of resignation for your current employer. The bottom line is that you're ready to seize the day.

Now you're on your way to the interview, and your car breaks down. You're hesitant to leave your car stranded on the side of a road, so you call for a tow truck. You may even call the potential employers to let them know you have been delayed. By the time the truck comes and tows your car away, you are extremely late for your interview. And when you reach the offices, you are informed that they needed to fill the position urgently and have offered the job to someone else.

At this point you're devastated because your expectations have been crushed. You expected to get the job, and now you don't have it. Your expectations not being met causes you immense unhappiness and dissatisfaction with life.

Three months later, you hear from a friend that the company you so desperately wanted to work for has now been sold, and the position you so badly wanted has been eliminated. You magically feel relieved and start counting your blessings. But what if you had skipped the drama when you didn't get the job and just counted your blessings? What if you had just said, "This job wasn't meant for me for a reason, and there's probably something better out there for me," and moved on? Don't you think that would have saved you three months of unhappiness? Accepting every situation as a blessing is very relaxing. A relaxed mind is a calm one, and a calm mind is a peaceful one.

This desire to be in control is the enemy of happiness. Embrace life as it comes, and stop trying to control it. Shooting for a particular outcome is human, but expecting it and tying your happiness to it is foolishness. Life could be a whole lot easier if we just went with the flow. Embrace all the things life has to offer without labeling them as "good" or "bad." Keep training your mind to embrace suboptimal situations. Assume positive intent when seemingly bad things happen to you. You are being given an opportunity to rise spiritually in these situations. In the words of Martin Luther King, Jr., "In a real sense, faith is total surrender to God."[5] **Acceptance and surrender are key attitudes that drive freedom and happiness.**

A Western journalist once asked Mahatma Gandhi the primary philosophy by which he led his life. He responded with "Renounce and enjoy," which was directly reflective of his spiritual leanings. Mahatma Gandhi was a student of Vedanta. The renunciation that Gandhi referred to was not the kind where you become a monk, renounce all material things, and head into seclusion. He was talking about renouncing expectations and attachment associated with all things that are inherently impermanent—that is, everything and everyone around you. It is the renunciation of the desire to control situations and the associated expectations. It is an acceptance of the attitude of surrender.

---

5. *The Papers of Martin Luther King, Jr., Volume VI: Advocate of the Social Gospel, September 1948–March 1963*, ed. Clayborne Carson (Berkeley, CA: University of California Press, 1992), 552.

EMBRACE CHOICELESS SITUATIONS

The bulk of the situations that we encounter in our lifetime are choiceless ones: our past (in this life or another), the present, the timing of our birth, who our parents are, being born into wealth or poverty, the people who come into our lives, the moment of our death. Even the choice of our life partner is considered choiceless and is based, rather, on which person is the right companion to enable our karmic journey. I realize that is a very bold statement to make. It doesn't mean you don't get to choose your life partner. What it means is that your "choice" is predetermined according to the nature of situations and experiences you need to encounter in this lifetime. The people who come into our lives, including our partners, are facilitators of those situations and experiences.

The law of karma tells us that situations are constantly presented to us on the basis of our past karma or actions. Just like in a play where we are actors, for a situation to be presented to us that is perfectly oriented to our needs, we need the right collaboration of actors to engage—our partners enabling our karmic journey while we are enabling theirs. Our free will is an important factor in the scheme of things and needs to be exercised, but it is only one factor among millions of others that drive the outcomes in our lives. Our future is determined by the karma we have created, but by the time it arrives it is the present and choiceless. This is why it is critical to live in the present and to accept every situation presented to us with the right attitude. Doing this generates the right kind of karma for the future. The American theologian Reinhold Niebuhr's famous Serenity Prayer, which is used in twelve-step programs, is very pertinent here: "God grant me the serenity to accept the things I cannot change, courage to change the things I can, and wisdom to know the difference."[6]

Change is another choiceless situation that if not embraced effectively can put a stranglehold on our happiness. Change is multifaceted in its impact, but let's look at it in two simplistic scenarios: change that impacts us directly and change that we want to see in other people who impact our happiness. Both these scenarios are choiceless.

In the first scenario, consider that we are going to constantly face change in our lives, whether it is a change to our physical bodies and appearance, our work, our family, the environment around us, or anything else. Some changes we perceive as positive, and others not so much. The positive ones we embrace, because they work in our favor. The negative ones cause us unhappiness.

Why do we let that happen to us? When someone we know is impacted by negative change—let's say a death in their family—the breadth of our verbal resilience is in full display. We hear ourselves tell them that change is the only thing that's permanent, their loved one is in a better place, and so on. Why don't those words and that resilience translate when the impacted party in question is us? Why is it that this deep spirituality—our ability to talk in terms of surrendering to God and acceptance—flows freely from our lips when we talk to others, but we get mired in a swamp of unhappiness when we experience something negative ourselves? Charles Darwin supposedly once said, referring to evolution, "It is not the strongest or the most intelligent who will survive, but those who can best manage change." I'm going to leverage the same message

---

6. *The Essential Reinhold Niebuhr: Selected Essays and Addresses*, ed. Robert McAfee Brown (New Haven, CT: Yale University Press, 1986), 251.

but replace the word *survive* with *be happy*. Happiness is a natural state for those who surrender to change.

Now, let's look at the second scenario regarding change. Say there's something very annoying about your spouse or friend or colleague, something this person does that you really can't stand. You're driving down the road, and you're thinking about this annoying trait, and it's making you more and more crazy. Suddenly another driver cuts you off, and you want to scream your lungs out at that driver for not knowing how to drive. If you had not been obsessing over how much you want this person to change an irritating habit, you would have reacted calmly or perhaps not even been cut off by the other driver.

I could go on and on with examples. We get frustrated with people because we want them to change to meet our needs. Here's the reality, though: people won't change unless they absolutely want to. The only way to stay mentally calm when you encounter these people you want to change is to *change yourself*. Don't let them get to you. Look the other way or, much better, just embrace them for who they are and tell yourself that in the broader scheme of things, your source of irritation is immaterial. This is a tough one, especially when it pertains to someone who is extremely close to you, like your spouse. **Embrace and surrender to all change that comes your way.**

When we accept that there are no coincidences in life, it is markedly easier to embrace and surrender to whatever life throws our way. Everything in this universe happens as it should—not just in the broader universe, but even within us, as each of us is a part of that universe. The human body is the perfect machine where everything happens as it should, and when something isn't happening appropriately, we get pertinent signals—for example, our body runs a fever when we have an infection. The same is the case with the universe. The story below is something I read online a while back and one that really resonated with me in terms of the mysterious ways in which the universe works.

The Doctor and His Faith

Dr. Mark, a well-known cancer specialist, was once on his way to an important conference in another city, where he was going to be honored with an award in the field of medical research. He was very excited to attend the conference and was desperate to reach it as soon as possible. However, two hours after the plane took off, it made an emergency landing at the nearest airport due to some technical snag. Afraid that he wouldn't make it in time for the conference, Dr. Mark immediately went to the reception counter and found that the next flight to the destination was not for ten hours. The receptionist suggested that he rent a car and drive down to the conference city, which was only a four-hour drive away. However, soon after he started, the weather suddenly changed, and a heavy storm began. The pouring rain made it very difficult to see the road, and he missed a turn he was supposed to take.

After some time, he finally came across a small tattered house. Desperate, he got out of the car and knocked on the door. A young lady opened the door. He explained the situation and asked her if he could use her telephone. However, the lady told him that she didn't have a phone or any electronic gadget, but she told him to come inside and wait till the weather improved. Hungry, wet, and exhausted, the doctor accepted her kind offer and walked in. The lady gave him hot tea and something to eat. The lady then requested he join her for prayer. But Dr. Mark smiled and said that he believed in hard work only and told her to continue with her prayers.

    Sitting on the chair, the doctor watched the woman sitting in the dim light of candles as she prayed next to what appeared to be a small baby crib. Every time she finished a prayer, she would start another one. Dr. Mark felt that the woman was in need of some help, and spoke to her as soon as she finished her prayers. The doctor asked her what exactly she wanted from God, and inquired if she thought God would ever listen to her prayers. He further asked about the small child in the crib for whom she was apparently praying. The lady gave a sad smile and said that the child in the crib was her son, who was suffering from a rare type of cancer, and there was only a doctor, called Mark, who could cure him. But she didn't have money to afford his fees, and moreover, Dr. Mark lived in another far-off town. She said that God would certainly answer her prayers one day and would create some way out, and added that she would not allow her fears to overcome her faith.

    Stunned and speechless, Dr. Mark was in tears. He whispered, "God is great . . . ," and recollected the sequence of events.

    There was a malfunction in the plane, a thunderstorm hit, and he lost his way. And all this happened because God not only just answered her prayers, but God also gave him a chance to come out of a materialistic world and spare some time to help the poor, hapless people, who have nothing but rich prayers!

ATTITUDE OF GRATITUDE

Piglet noticed that even though he had a very small heart, it could hold rather a large amount of gratitude.
—A. A. Milne, *Winnie-the-Pooh*[7]

We have so much to be grateful for in this life, yet it takes a lot for the words *thank you* to cross our lips on a consistent basis. The fact that you are reading this means you can see, you are alive, you can comprehend—all important things to be very grateful for. We spend so much of our lives complaining about things around us, or finding faults with other people, or whining about things we don't have, or in general being unhappy.

When Zoey was diagnosed with DIPG, she was unable to join her kindergarten class, even though she was enrolled, because she was going to undergo radiation treatment. She had been really looking forward to starting kindergarten, and we were forced to tell her that she couldn't go because she had a boo-boo in her head. One day, while we were driving together, she noticed that I was crying and asked me the reason for my tears. I told her that I was angry with God for giving her a boo-boo in her head. She said I was missing the point—God didn't give her the boo-boo; he was taking it away. It was a clear message that in her mind we should be thanking God for helping her with her boo-boo. She passed away three months later, and God took care of her boo-boo by taking it away and not letting it bother her anymore.

If a five-year-old with a boo-boo in her head, double vision, and an unstable gait who was going through radiation with a mask on her face could find it in her heart to be grateful, why would it be so hard for the rest of us? We are conditioned to focus on what's not working in our lives instead of what is.

---

7. A. A. Milne, *Winnie-the-Pooh* (London: Methuen & Co. Ltd., 1926).

THE HAPPINESS MODEL

We find a reason to complain about everything that doesn't meet our arbitrary expectations. It may be the weather, people, God... nothing is off-limits. There's a great story that I want to share here, about a teacher imparting an important life lesson to his class.

The Black Dot

One day, a professor entered his classroom and asked his students to prepare for a surprise test. They all waited anxiously at their desks for the exam to begin.

The professor handed out the exams, and to everyone's surprise, there were no questions—just a black dot in the center of the paper. The professor, seeing the expression on everyone's faces, told them the following: "I want you to write about what you see there."

The students, confused, got started working on the task at hand.

At the end of the class, the professor took all the exams and started reading each one of them out loud in front of all the students. All of them, without exception, defined the black dot, trying to explain its position in the center of the sheet.

After all the class responses had been read, the professor started to explain. "I'm not going to grade you on this; I just wanted to give you something to think about. No one wrote about the white part of the paper. Everyone focused on the black dot—and the same thing happens in our lives. We insist on focusing only on the black dot—the health issues that bother us, the lack of money, the complicated relationship with a family member, etc. The dark spots are very small when compared to everything we have in our lives, but they are the ones that taint our minds and steal our focus. Take your eyes away from the black dots in your lives. Enjoy each one of your blessings, each moment that life gives you. Be happy and live a life filled with love!"

That is how we are conditioned, to see the black dots in our lives and not the beautiful white paper that surrounds them. Yet we have friends to lean on, families who love us, work that provides us with our livelihood and our financial means, earth that provides us with food, rain to ease the heat, the sun's warmth to ease the chill of winter, the cackle of children to remind us of simpler times . . . I could go on and on. We essentially have so much to be grateful for. Self-pity is draining and depressing. It creates nothing but negative energy. We don't just bring ourselves down, but also the people around us.

According to the National Institutes of Health (NIH), "the majority of empirical studies indicate that there is a direct association between gratitude and a sense of overall well-being."[8] Robert Emmons, a professor of psychology at UC Davis, has exhaustively researched the benefits of gratitude. His results show that gratitude has the following benefits:

- physical—stronger immune systems, lower blood pressure, better sleep
- psychological—higher levels of positive emotions, more optimism and happiness
- social—more helpful, generous, and compassionate; more forgiving; less lonely and isolated[9]

---

8. Randy A. Sansone and Lori A. Sansone, "Gratitude and Well Being: The Benefits of Appreciation," *Psychiatry* (Edgmont) 7, no. 11 (2010): 18–22.
9. Robert A. Emmons and Michael E. McCullough, "Counting Blessings

Is it easy being thankful when confronted with seemingly suboptimal or bad situations? No, it isn't. But this is where inner attitude comes into play. We can choose to be thankful. We can choose positivity over self-pity. We can choose to stop whining, and when we feel the urge to complain, we can say a quiet "Thank you" instead to quell the feeling. It takes a lot of very deliberate practice, but I can say from my own experience it is well worth it. Not giving in to negative thoughts and just thanking the universe (God) for whatever comes our way is a sure-shot recipe for inner peace and happiness. Let's take a moment today to put all our complaints and concerns on the shelf and just say "Thank you." Let's choose to live our lives with an attitude of gratitude.

Versus Burdens: An Experimental Investigation of Gratitude and Subjective Well-Being in Daily Life," *Journal of Personality and Social Psychology* 84, no. 2 (2003): 377–89.

CHAPTER 4

PRINCIPLE 3: PERFORM ACTIONS WITHOUT EXPECTATIONS AND WITH GRATITUDE

Up to this point, we have discussed two principles. Principle 1 says that we are all primarily on a spiritual journey and need to focus on making forward progress toward our goal. Everything else is secondary, and when we embrace that idea, we are fully committed to addressing our desire for inner peace. Principle 2 focuses on the attitude of surrender and the acceptance of everything that comes our way as a blessing. The attitude of acceptance or surrender, in tandem with a feeling of gratitude to God, helps cleanse our minds of the habit of labeling our experiences "good" or "bad," which triggers mental disturbance. Embracing the second principle allows our minds to be peaceful.

Principle 3 is based on having the right attitude when performing actions. "Clear eyes, full hearts—can't lose": this was the fictional coach Eric Taylor's message to his football players in one of my favorite TV shows, *Friday Night Lights*. He was essentially saying that if you play the game with integrity and give it your 100 percent, you can never lose, irrespective of the game's outcome. What an incredible message when applied to everything in life. If you give everything you undertake your 100 percent and perform those actions with a clean heart and mind, you are always a winner, you are always comfortable with yourself, and you are always happy.

If you've been following each principle of *The Happiness Model* closely, perhaps you've noticed that my emphasis over and over again is about changing your attitude. In this case, I am urging you to assume the attitude that you will do your very best and let the outcome be whatever it may be. When you play a sport, play it to your fullest, leaving nothing behind. When you love somebody, give that person your all, and don't worry if your heart might be broken. When you go to work, do the best job you possibly can. Have an attitude of no regrets, an attitude that ensures your conscience will always be clear because you have done right by the gifts and talents that have been given to you and have left nothing behind on the table. Give life your 100 percent even when no one else is looking . . . because *you* are looking.

If we embrace this practice of giving 100 percent to whatever we do while being grateful to God for giving us the ability to perform the action to our fullest, we will be able to drive unhappiness out of our lives. Being grateful to God for what we receive (Principle 2) and grateful as well for our ability to perform (Principle 3) is an extremely important attitude for sustained inner peace, happiness, and equanimity (Principle 5). The second principle teaches us an important lesson in managing expectations by embracing whatever comes our way. In

Principle 3, the ask is that we perform our actions to the best possible extent without getting hung up on the outcome and the associated expectations.

In Principle 1 we discussed how spiritual development includes an understanding that we are entitled only to our actions and not their outcomes. That construct directly correlates to Principle 3. If we need to have a sense of entitlement, let's direct that sense toward the quality of our actions in everything we do. Being the best parent we can possibly be does not mean our kids turn out to be the best versions of ourselves. How our kids end up is out of our control; we are entitled only to doing our best as parents. Similarly, on the work front, we are entitled to putting our best foot forward professionally, but that doesn't mean every one of us will experience professional greatness. Performing our actions with a sense of gratitude, duty, or purpose gives us tremendous inner peace and happiness, irrespective of the outcome.

When we talk about a gratitude-filled action orientation, we're talking about every facet of the environment that impacts our lives and mental health. We've discussed our personal and professional lives, but the people around us—whether we interact with them regularly or come across them briefly—impact us as well. It is as important to be true to Principle 3 in our interactions with those around us as it is to be true to ourselves. I'd like to discuss next how our attitude toward others impacts our own sense of peace and happiness.

ACTIONS TOWARD OTHERS

Have you ever tried being good to others and not expecting anything in return? The feeling is amazing. We are all inherently good people, but our expectations of others get in the way of our acting on that goodness. What if we just thanked

God for the fact that there are people in our lives and demonstrated that gratitude by being good to them? Good intentions and actions toward others without any expectations in return is a fantastic recipe for happiness. This doesn't pertain just to our inner circle of family and friends, but also much more broadly to the people we come across in our lives. Please keep in mind here that the law of karma is a live measuring stick in every one of our interactions; it gauges both our intent and actions. When we help an elderly person across the street, donate money to a charity out of the goodness of our hearts (and not because it is a tax deduction), treat people who are less fortunate than ourselves with kindness and respect, or are polite to a customer service person at the other end of a phone line, we are performing actions with an attitude of gratitude. Here's an abbreviated version of a story by Paul Villiard that drives home this point.

Information Please

When I was quite young, my father had one of the first telephones in our neighborhood. I remember well the polished old case fastened to the wall. The shiny receiver hung on the side of the box. I was too little to reach the telephone, but used to listen with fascination when my mother talked to it. Then I discovered that somewhere inside the wonderful device lived an amazing person—her name was "Information Please," and there was nothing she did not know. "Information Please" could supply anybody's number and the correct time.

My first personal experience with this genie in the bottle came one day while my mother was visiting a neighbor. Amusing myself at the tool bench in the basement, I whacked my finger with a hammer. The pain was terrible, but there didn't seem to be any reason for crying because there was no one home to give sympathy. I walked around the house sucking my throbbing finger, finally arriving at the stairway. The telephone! Quickly, I ran for the footstool in the parlor and dragged it to the landing. Climbing up, I unhooked the receiver and held it to my ear. "Information Please," I said into the mouthpiece just above my head.

A click or two and a small clear voice spoke into my ear, "Information."

"I hurt my finger," I wailed into the phone. The tears came readily enough now that I had an audience.

"Isn't your mother home?" came the question.

"Nobody's home but me," I blubbered.

"Are you bleeding?" the voice asked.

"No," I replied. "I hit my finger with the hammer, and it hurts."

"Can you open your icebox?" she asked.

I said I could.

"Then chip off a little piece of ice and hold it to your finger," said the voice.

After that, I called "Information Please" for everything. I asked her for help with my geography, and she told me where Philadelphia was. She helped me with my math. She told me my pet chipmunk, which I had caught in the park just the day before, would eat fruit and nuts. When our pet canary, Petey, died, "Information Please" was there for me. I asked her, "Why is it that birds should sing so beautifully and bring joy to all families, only to end up as a heap of feathers on the bottom of a cage?"

She must have sensed my deep concern, for she said quietly, "Paul, always remember that there are other worlds to sing in." Somehow, I felt better.

All this took place in a small town in the Pacific Northwest. When I was nine years old, we moved across the country to Boston. I missed my friend very much. "Information Please" belonged in that old wooden box back home, and I somehow never thought of trying the tall, skinny new phone that sat on the table in the hall.

As I grew into my teens, the memories of those childhood conversations never really left me. Often, in moments of doubt and perplexity, I would recall the serene sense of security I had then. I appreciated now how patient, understanding, and kind she was to have spent her time on a little boy.

A few years later, on my way west to college, my plane put down in Seattle. I had about half an hour or so between planes. I spent fifteen minutes on the phone with my sister, who lived there now. Then, without thinking what I was doing, I dialed my hometown operator and said, "Information Please."

Miraculously, I heard the small, clear voice I knew so well: "Information."

I hadn't planned this, but I heard myself saying, "Could you please tell me how to spell fix?"

There was a long pause. Then came the soft-spoken answer: "I guess your finger must have healed by now."

I laughed. "So, it's really still you," I said. "I wonder if you have any idea how much you meant to me during that time."

"I wonder," she said, "if you know how much your calls meant to me. I never had any children, and I used to look forward to your calls."

I told her how often I had thought of her over the years, and I asked if I could call her again when I came back to visit my sister.

"Please do," she said. "Just ask for Sally."

Three months later I was back in Seattle. A different voice answered, "Information." I asked for Sally.

"Are you a friend?" she asked.

"Yes, a very old friend," I answered.

"I'm sorry to have to tell you this," she said. "Sally has been working part-time the last few years because she was sick. She died five weeks ago."

Before I could hang up she said, "Wait a minute. Did you say your name was Paul?"

"Yes," I replied.

"Well, Sally left a message for you. She wrote it down in case you called. Let me read it to you." The note said, "Tell him I still say there are other worlds to sing in. He'll know what I mean."

I thanked her and hung up. I knew what Sally meant.[10]

Isn't that a beautiful story? Never reject an opportunity to make a difference in someone's life, even if it feels like you're going out of your way. Perform your actions with a sense of humility and gratitude, even those actions that are associated with people you don't know or haven't met personally. How good do you feel after a rude conversation with a customer service representative? The people on the other end of the line are

---

10. Adapted from Paul Villiard, "The Voice in the Box," *Reader's Digest*, June 1966.

just trying to do their job at a fairly low wage level. The experience of someone speaking respectfully or kindly to them over the phone is enough to put a smile on their faces. Having run a customer service operation in the past, I know how valuable a respectful or kind customer call is to the morale and psyche of the representative.

There's another story that touched me deeply when I read it and is directly related to performing actions with a sense of respect and gratitude, knowing that every action of ours that touches someone else has the ability to leave a mark.

Grandma and Her Pencil

Once upon a time, a boy was watching his grandmother write a letter. At one point, he asked, "Are you writing a story about what we've done? Is it a story about me?"

His grandmother stopped writing her letter and said to her grandson, "I am writing about you, actually, but more important than the words is the pencil I'm using. I hope you will be like this pencil when you grow up."

Intrigued, the boy looked at the pencil. It didn't seem very special. "But it's just like any other pencil I've ever seen!" he said.

"That depends on how you look at things," the grandmother replied. "This pencil has five qualities that, if you manage to hang on to them, will make you a person who is always at peace with the world.

"First quality: You are capable of great things, but you must never forget that there is a hand guiding your steps. We call that hand God, and he always guides us according to his will.

"Second quality: Now and then, I have to stop writing and use a sharpener. That makes the pencil suffer a little, but afterward, he's much sharper. So you, too, must learn to bear certain pains and sorrows, because they will make you a better person.

"Third quality: The pencil always allows us to use an eraser to rub out any mistakes. This means that correcting something we did is not necessarily a bad thing; it helps to keep us on the road to justice.

"Fourth quality: What really matters in a pencil is not its wooden exterior, but the graphite inside. So always pay attention to what is happening inside you.

"Finally, the pencil's fifth quality: It always leaves a mark. In just the same way, you should know that everything you do in life will leave a mark, so try to be conscious of that in your every action."[11]

The message in this story is beautiful and touches on some extremely important life lessons that assist with our spiritual development. The first and last qualities are the ones that directly pertain to the principle of performing actions with gratitude, because they teach us to embrace and be thankful for the knowledge that God is guiding our gifts and our ability to maximize those gifts. Even the fact that we are able to use a pencil to perform the action of writing is worthy of gratitude, because that same action would be incredibly challenging to a person with no arms or someone with rheumatoid arthritis. Never take anything for granted. You have been given the ability to do good for others. Be thankful for that gift, and

---

11. Paulo Coelho, "The Story of the Pencil," in *Like the Flowing River: Stories 1998–2005*, trans. Margaret Jull Costa (New York: Madison Park Press, 2006).

acknowledge it by doing the right things for others with the right attitude of gratitude.

ACTIONS TOWARD YOUR FAMILY

In the era of smartphones and high-stress jobs, we seem to spend our entire time multitasking and not really focusing on the one area of our personal lives that needs our 100 percent: our families. We are both texting and driving; we are working while we're at home with the kids; we're talking to our spouse but thinking about that situation at work; we're trying to watch our kids play soccer but are distracted by the one other thing we need to take care of that has eluded us all day . . . you get the idea.

With Zoey, I attempted to be an extremely engaged father and tried to maximize the time we had together on weekends and weeknights. When she passed, I thought I would have a bunch of "if I had more time" thoughts, but found that I didn't. In a moment of contemplation, I asked myself why that was the case and why I was completely at peace and happy with the time we did have. The answer was very clear: focusing on her when I was with her and maximizing our time together had taken away any regrets and associated unhappiness. That's when the criticality of focused engagement in our kids' lives struck me. Maybe the intuitive feeling that I was running out of time with Zoey gave me the ability to offer her my undivided attention. Whether that's why or not, I do realize that it was the right thing to do. My wife, Zoey, and I had taken a lot of family vacations together, including trips to Florida (SeaWorld, Disney), Barcelona, Hilton Head, Saint Louis (so she could see the home where she was born), and a host of other places. While we obviously never planned it that way, and even thinking along these lines would have been ludicrous, we had filled the five and a half years we had with our little girl with a lifetime of memories.

Our families and especially our kids are a major source of happiness in our lives, yet we constantly choose to focus on other things like work, money, and so on. We keep putting off things we want to do together as a family because we take for granted that time is always going to be on our side. We assume our family unit will be intact next year for that trip that we can't take this year because there's an important project under way at work. Don't take life for granted, and especially don't take your family for granted. Make them a clear priority. Give your family your 100 percent attention, and always prioritize them ahead of everything else. When the going gets tough, you can nearly always rely on your family to stand by you. I realize that I'm generalizing here a bit, but I'm going to be optimistic and stay with the thought that most families would rise to the occasion when needed.

When Zoey was diagnosed with DIPG, members of our family gave us their 100 percent without any expectations. We had both sets of grandparents around us for support. My aunt from Boston dropped everything she had going on and moved to our home during Zoey's radiation treatments so that she could drive Zoey to the hospital. Zoey's aunt and uncle from Dallas were with us through the last couple of weeks, ready to help if we needed something from a store or pharmacy. On numerous occasions I tried to thank them, but they would say they were just grateful to have the opportunity to help and to spend time with Zoey. Their attitude perfectly showcases Principle 3. Even to this day, when I call my aunt to thank her for everything she did for us, she reiterates that she feels extremely blessed God gave her the opportunity to be there for Zoey, and that the knowledge that she was able to help gives her more mental satisfaction and peace than most other experiences in her life. Maximize your time with your family and friends; take the attitude that if something unexpected were to happen, you would have no regrets.

STOP BEING JUDGMENTAL

A major barrier inhibits our ability to derive inner peace from performing actions with gratitude, and that barrier is our innate pull toward judging others. Think about all you've read in this chapter regarding performing actions to the best possible extent, without expectations, and with gratitude to God for giving you the ability to perform them. Now think about how that applies to the stakeholders in your life: your family, friends, other people around you, your boss, and so forth. Are there some people with whom we balk at applying Principle 3? Sometimes we find ourselves making excuses for why Principle 3 doesn't work in every situation because of the varied nature of the people we interact with. Essentially, we've judged them as being unworthy of our action-oriented gratitude.

We are very quick to create a negative opinion of people when our interaction with them is suboptimal, but very slow to change that opinion when our interactions are positive. And our judging doesn't stop with one interaction. Once we've created a black or white impression of the person in our minds, we keep applying the same impression to every interaction with that person. We never take the time to think that others may be judging us as well while we're in the midst of being judgmental. Being quick to judge others is not a good quality, and we are all inherently good people. When we realize we have misread a person and thought incorrectly of them, we are the most disappointed in ourselves. Why waste our energy judging others when we can so often be wrong? Here are two short stories that exemplify why judging others is not a value-added behavior and does nothing to promote inner peace.

The Man Child

A twenty-four-year-old boy looking out from the train's window shouted, "Dad, look, the trees are going behind!"

Dad smiled, and a young couple sitting nearby looked at the twenty-four-year-old's childish behavior with pity.

Suddenly he again exclaimed, "Dad, look, the clouds are running with us!"

The couple couldn't resist and said to the boy's father, "Why don't you take your son to a good doctor?"

The father smiled and said, "I did, and we are just coming from the hospital. My son was blind from birth; he just got his eyes today."

Beware of Quick Judgment

There is an old Welsh fable told of a dog that had belonged to Llywelyn the Great, a prince of Gwynedd in the thirteenth century. He had been given the dog as a gift from King John of England. Prince Llywelyn's wife had passed away, and the dog was charged with watching the cradle of the prince's baby when he went hunting. After one particular hunting trip, the prince had returned home to find the cradle of the baby overturned and the bedding and the floor covered in blood.

With the baby missing and seeing his dog's mouth covered with blood, the prince took out his sword and killed the dog, thinking that it had killed the baby. The dog's dying yelp was answered by a child's cry. The prince searched and found the baby unharmed, lying near the dead body of a wolf. The dog had actually been protecting the baby as its owner had desired. The prince was filled with such remorse that he never smiled again.[12]

In all candor, shedding the automatic instinct to judge others was and continues to be one of the tougher aspects of my spiritual journey. The method that I've found especially useful is to ask myself if I would ever want to be in the other person's shoes without knowing everything about them. Without knowing the Zoey backstory, all people see when they interact with Suman and me is a couple who are financially comfortable and have two adorable little boys. Most people would walk away from that interaction with the judgment that our lives are idyllic. They don't realize that every memorable family moment in our lives is now tinged with the "if she were here" thought. They can't comprehend what it is to watch your older boy turn five and have some of the same conversations you had with your five-year-old girl before she fell sick. They don't know what it feels like to have a sense of déjà vu, only to realize wistfully that you will never see the other person you had that conversation with again in this lifetime. They don't realize or comprehend any of these things because they're not walking in our shoes or living in our minds.

Try this technique the next time you find yourself judging people: ask yourself if you'd want to be in their shoes without knowing everything about them; assume they might have challenges in their lives that dwarf yours in comparison. You will

---

12. As quoted in "Be Careful of Being Judgmental—Great Story," Michael Rogers, *Teamwork and Leadership*, November 2012, http://www.teamworkandleadership.com/2012/11/be-careful-of-being-judgmental-great-story.html.

THE HAPPINESS MODEL

automatically start feeling a sense of empathy and respect in your interactions with others.

BE A GIVER, NOT A TAKER

Givers are always trying to figure out what they can do for others. "How can I be of assistance?" is the foremost thought for a giver. A taker is always trying to figure out how to gain something from the situation. A giver is spiritually developed, while a taker is not. A giver listens more than a taker. Givers want to make a difference, while takers want to understand what's in it for them. Givers see God in people and the things around them, while takers are always seeking attention. Givers give their 100 percent and are always willing to help someone else, whereas takers don't give their all and then whine about their schedules. Givers enrich the lives of the people they meet and make people around them happy, while takers can be draining. Givers are happy people, while takers are not.

Be a giver, not a taker. Givers create happiness for themselves and others around them.

The Giving Tree by Shel Silverstein is, in my view, one of the best childhood stories ever written, with a beautiful way of showcasing a giver and a taker. If you haven't read this one before, I highly recommend picking up a copy. It is a story about the interactions between a tree and a boy. The boy is a taker and constantly wants things from the Giving Tree. When he's little, he wants to climb the tree and play on it. When he grows a little older, he takes the apples the tree produces and sells them to make money, and the tree happily gives him what he desires. When he grows older still and needs wood to build a house, he comes back to the tree with another ask, and the tree gladly offers its branches to him to cut down. This taking from the boy and the giving from the tree continues until the boy becomes an old man, and all that's left of the tree is a stump for him to rest on. The story is brilliant and teaches us an extremely important life lesson: there is happiness in giving and sadness in taking.

DO WHAT YOU ARE SUPPOSED TO DO IN THIS LIFETIME

We are all born with certain abilities, and the way we can show gratitude to God for what we've been given is to maximize the usage of those gifts and abilities. Performing actions to 100 percent of your potential becomes markedly easier when you are doing things that come naturally to you and are in sync with your innate abilities.

Most of us work an eight-to-five workday and start the week mentally waiting for the weekend to come. We work at jobs that we are passionless about and that mean nothing more to us than a paycheck. We are good at what we do, and we feel that is good enough—not good enough to be happy, but rather good enough to enable us to save some money for our retirement. We essentially tell ourselves that happiness is a luxury we will think about after we retire, because striving for happiness prior to that is too much work. But what if we get terminally ill and never make it to retirement, or something else happens and life is cut short? Life is not predictable enough for us to postpone happiness to a later date.

Many of us don't take the time to figure out if we are doing what we are supposed to in this lifetime. What comes naturally to us? What do we love doing? What we love to do is what we should be doing. That may seem naive to some, but here's a fact: if you do what you love, it ceases to feel like work. As I reflected on the jobs I've had over the last ten years as an executive at companies of various sizes, I came to realize that helping others develop their careers and helping them with life's challenges was a passion of mine, and it seemed that people gravitated naturally toward me for coaching. While I continued to maximize my role as a leader and coach in the workplace, earlier this year I decided that I needed to make that passion real and start a coaching practice. So, this past summer, I quit my job and put all my attention on building a company focused on life and executive coaching. I plan to head back into the workplace in due course and continue my passion for developing leaders there, but this coaching business, through which I can make a meaningful difference in people's lives, will always be there for me. If nothing else, I will not have any regrets about not pursuing my passion.

There's a reason I wanted to share my personal story with you on this topic. This isn't about quitting your job and chasing after your dreams, which is not a realistic choice for most people. This is about finding the things in your life that give you happiness and figuring out a way to make time for them. This is about enjoying all of the journey that is life, rather than expecting the fun part of it to pick up when you're perhaps too old to enjoy it. This is about ensuring that you do what makes you happy today and don't put it off. All you are guaranteed is this moment. Embrace this moment for what it is—a gift. Make the most of this moment with your God-given abilities. Doing that is how you can demonstrate your gratitude for the abilities that you've been given.

CHAPTER 5

PRINCIPLE 4:
MANAGE YOUR EGO

After mismanaged expectations, the "because of me" syndrome is a close second in the race among drivers of unhappiness. The notion that wonderful things happen because we are in control of them and our brilliance somehow made them a reality is utterly foolish. There is nothing wrong with being very confident, but nothing good comes from having the perspective that things happened only because of you.

On the flip side, tempering this perspective and appreciating that your contributions and skills were only one factor among many that made something happen is a great driver of happiness. For everything we achieve in life, a multitude of factors needs to be executed to perfection. Every role we play in our lives is dependent on other people for success.

Even as an amazing golfer, Tiger Woods, who played an individual sport that in theory should solely depend on one's abilities, needed more than his incredible skills to be successful. Imperfect weather conditions or a bad back, as was the case with him, could completely derail his brilliance. All people, no matter how good they are at what they do, need multiple elements to play nicely in the sandbox together for the desired outcome to be achieved. Many, many of these factors are things we can't control. All the greatest self-help gurus in the world—those people who tell you that when you put your mind to something, plan for it, and then execute, nothing can stop you from achieving your goals—are clearly not talking about cancer and the debilitating effects it can have on not only the patient but also the family that decides to take it on. I was always of the belief that I could accomplish anything and that everything in life was possible with a goal in mind and a plan to make it happen—that is, until Zoey was diagnosed with an inoperable brain tumor. Even the best-laid plans would not have worked for her. There is arguably no better place in the world than the US to be diagnosed with pediatric cancer, because if there is a cure for that specific kind of cancer, it is more likely than not that one of the leading children's hospitals in the US will be able to treat it. In a lot of ways, Zoey's diagnosis and eventual passing were the greatest lessons in humility for Suman and me as parents.

The entire "because of me" syndrome, which boosts our ego, needs to be reconsidered, and our thinking needs to change to drive inner peace. Whatever happened was because a multitude of other things worked as expected to ensure your desired outcome was achieved. Vedanta refers to the multitude of external factors that contributed to your success as God as well. Additionally, God gave you the skills to make it happen. We need to replace the "because of me" thought process with "because of God and with my effort included."

The "because of me" syndrome also brings with it a level of arrogance and heightened expectations. Our ego gets significantly bolstered when we believe things happen because of us, and that is reflected in how we interact with people. We start feeling that we are in complete control and can make things happen without needing other people. People become a commodity in our lives. When we think of people as a commodity, we don't consistently treat them well or don't treat them well at all. When we don't treat others well, the natural tendency is that they don't respect us and treat us well either. We are all inherently good—after all, there is godliness in each one of us—but when we treat people poorly, we start to lose respect for ourselves and turn progressively more negative toward naysayers. This negativity creates bad karma for ourselves. When people respond to our behavior and treat us poorly back, it affects our ability to eat, sleep, and most importantly, find happiness in this world.

OUR EGO IS A MAJOR CAUSE OF UNHAPPINESS

According to Vedanta, the fundamental reason we have an ego is because we identify with our physical self (our physical body and mental strengths) instead of our spiritual self. While growing up, we are naturally trained to think of life in terms of wins and losses, and the additional orientation to our physical selves makes this a highly superficial game of "I won this, because of me." The superficial nature of our thinking about our successes as a direct reflection of our physical abilities prevents us from thinking deeper about the reasons for our success.

In the first principle, we had discussed that we are spiritual beings rather than physical ones. Being a spiritual being and understanding spirituality to be our eventual goal would require us to look at life's dualities with a much deeper perspective. When we have incredible winnings in the stock market, it is because of our brilliance, but when we lose a ton of money, it is because the market was unfavorable. Our tendency to deflect our losses and gloat over our wins demonstrates an inherent inability to accept two things: Firstly, winning and losing are temporary phenomena and should be treated as such. Secondly, we don't play games to lose, and there were countless additional factors that contributed to the winning or losing, in addition to our abilities and the effort we put into the enterprise. Our strong belief that our abilities and effort solely contribute to our wins and losses is why we have unwarranted highs and lows that impact our inner peace.

TAKING ON MORE THAN WE CAN HANDLE

How many times in life have we found that we have bitten off more than we can chew? We feel like something is done right only when it is done a certain way, and we, magically, are the only people who know that way. Our feeling that something gets done right only when we do it is based on our ego as well. While this perfectionism doesn't come across with the same negative force as self-centeredness, it still has some very consistent patterns. If we look at it dispassionately, we've taken on more than we can or should handle, which stresses us out; we've ticked off a bunch of people who dislike this trait in us; and we've collectively created unhappiness for ourselves and the people around us. After all that, even if we did do a very good job with whatever we were trying to accomplish, no one cares.

We need to learn to let go. The tighter we try to hold on to something, the more detrimental it becomes to our mental well-being. This applies to both people and work. Letting go gives us freedom, alleviates stress, allows others to prove themselves, and creates happiness all around. From a personal standpoint, I can tell you that understanding that you don't need to carry yourself and everyone around you on your back—that you can just let go—is an incredible stress reliever.

The more you take on, the more stressed you get, and the more worries and unhappiness you create. Train yourself to let go.

As you can well imagine, the notion of letting go is easy enough in concept but a tough one to execute. The reason it is tough to execute is because we have internalized the belief that only we can get it right. I was watching the first season of the Netflix series *The Crown* a couple of weeks ago, and they do a masterful job in that show of showcasing how Winston Churchill, arguably one of the greatest leaders of the twentieth century and the architect of Hitler's defeat in World War II, struggled with letting go. He was eighty and still believed that no one else would be able to handle the job of being the British prime minister better than him.

Here's how I've trained myself to master this over the years. Professionally, I've always ingrained in myself the perspective that my job is to put myself out of a job—that is, to enable someone else to do it so I can move on to other things. This would help the other person grow as well, which is a win-win outcome. On the personal front, the perfectionist in me has struggled with letting go, but over the years I've found it to be an invaluable way to create more time for me to focus on my reading and writing. Practice letting go by starting small; then keep walking away from more and more and see how it feels. Letting go is both therapeutic and strangely relieving; it is a great way to feel lighter and more at peace with the world. The following story resonated with me as I thought about pulling closer versus letting go.

The Weight of the Glass

A psychology professor walked around on a stage while teaching stress-management principles to an auditorium filled with students. She raised a glass of water and asked, "How heavy is this glass of water I'm holding?"

Students shouted out answers ranging from eight ounces to a couple of pounds.

She replied, "From my perspective, the absolute weight of this glass doesn't matter. It all depends on how long I hold it. If I hold it for a minute or two, it's fairly light. If I hold it for an hour straight, its weight might make my arm ache a little. If I hold it for a day straight, my arm will likely cramp up and feel completely numb and paralyzed, forcing me to drop the glass to the floor. In each case, the weight of the glass doesn't change, but the longer I hold it, the heavier it feels to me." As the class nodded their heads in agreement, she continued, "Your stresses and worries in life are very much like this glass of water. Think about them for a while, and nothing happens. Think about them a bit longer, and you begin to ache a little. Think about them all day long, and you will feel completely numb and paralyzed—incapable of doing anything else until you drop them."

TREAT OTHERS WITH RESPECT

Our ego gets in the way of treating others with respect. We get caught up in the feeling that we need to get respect to give respect. When people interact with us, we are constantly monitoring their body language as well as their words to ensure they are treating us appropriately before we will deign to give them respect. Many of us don't naturally assume positive intent and are constantly reading between the lines. This constant cycle of conversation monitoring and measuring our givebacks is tiring and creates a lot of negativity within us. The negativity causes us unhappiness and results in our treating the other person poorly, and so the cycle continues.

We should take a page from the observation of Maya Angelou, the famous American poet and civil rights activist: "I've learned that people will forget what you said, people will forget what you did, but people will never forget how you made them feel." It doesn't take much out of us to treat others with respect and compassion. It is not material whether you like the person or not. The message here is not that we should like everyone, which I realize borders on the impossible, but rather that treating others with respect creates positive energy. Positive energy can only create happiness for ourselves and those around us. Negative energy is not good for us in the karmic sense; when we create it, it means we will need to keep encountering those kinds of situations and people until we are spiritually evolved enough to handle them in a positive fashion and with respect. Treating people the way you would like to be treated creates more positive energy both within you and in the world around you.

EGO VERSUS SELF-CONFIDENCE AND RETAINING YOUR POWER

Tremendous self-confidence is most often misconstrued to be an elevated ego. If a person is very confident about something and has a strong opinion about it, the people around that person see that self-confidence as a sign of an inflated ego. I've encountered that multiple times in my career. It used to bother me tremendously, until the principles of Vedanta helped me take a step back and realize that the perspectives other people had could only bother me if I let them. The sole opinion about you that matters is yours, because you have to live with yourself and your choices. If you are on the right path spiritually and are doing the right things by your conscience, you need not worry about what other people think. You can only control yourself, not others.

A good way to differentiate self-confidence from an inflated ego is to assess what each of them does to our mental peace. If, in a certain situation, things don't go the way a confident person expects them to, he or she doesn't feel beaten up; the confident person responds by trying harder, by assuming the right attitude, or by simply walking away. In either case, the confidence and positive follow-through are intact. You need to feel confident in yourself, what you bring to the table, and your actions. Having that level of self-confidence will give you a sense of freedom from others, and as a result others will not be able to cause you any unhappiness.

Ego-driven people, on the other hand, take the suboptimal result very personally and drag both themselves and others around them down as a result of their attitude. I've seen this happen to extremely strong personalities, and it is unfortunate that one would unwittingly choose a path of unhappiness and mental strife. Control your ego, because if it's not managed, it is a driver of great unhappiness. Conversely, don't give others the power to make you feel a certain way about yourself; you need to retain that power fully. There's a clear line between feeling good about yourself—filled with confidence—and having an unmanaged ego. Only you can be the judge of when you've crossed that line, based on how you feel and react.

THE IMPORTANCE OF EGO MANAGEMENT

Constantly seeking the approval of others is a clear indication that you are ego driven. No one else's opinion of you matters as much as your own. However, it is important to realize that you're not always right. The feeling that you're always right is another sure sign that you're ego driven and that your ego needs tempering. Being self-confident and not seeking the approval of others does not mean that it is OK to feel that only you are right and the opinions of others don't matter. Self-confident people are in fact more welcoming of others' perspectives, because they understand that discussions are not about winning or losing and that other, possibly even better, perspectives do not reflect poorly on them. Egotists will see every conversation as a test of their smarts, and when things don't go as expected, they end up being disillusioned or unhappy.

We need to change our thinking and our attitude about ourselves in order to be peaceful. We need to think of "by the grace of God" or "thanks to the universe" as the starting point of our victories, clearly acknowledging to ourselves that something much bigger than us was in play for the outcome to be successful. While our skills and talents might be very sound and we may be able to push toward a certain outcome, a successful completion is always because of something much bigger than us.

As I take a step back and think about this journey that I'm on, it is easy enough to focus on the rearview mirror and feel good about the progress I have made. However, I understand and appreciate full well that I have a very long way to go, and none of this would have been possible without other key people in my life: Zoey as my guide and conscience; my Vedanta guru (teacher) in India, who continues to help me uncover the depths of this philosophy and better understand God; God, who blessed me with grace and the intellectual capacity to internalize new concepts and gave me the strength to make these principles an inherent part of my life; and Suman, who has been incredibly supportive every step along the way and has given me the space to find my path. Without these, this journey could very easily have been a nonevent.

Shedding our ego is incredibly hard. We are naturally comfortable with thinking of ourselves as better than everybody else. Why else would we pass judgment on others? There are some self-help gurus who will challenge my suggestion to drop the ego. Their perspective is that you keep feeding the ego, mentally telling yourself that you are better than everyone else, and then chase your dreams. My point here is not that I am against mentally bolstering our can-do attitude, nor that I believe we should undermine ourselves in any way. We all have amazing talents that are our responsibility to groom and showcase. Do it with humility, though. Think of yourself as a means to an end rather than the end itself.

CHAPTER 6

PRINCIPLE 5: BUILD EQUANIMITY

The *Oxford English Dictionary* defines *equanimity* as "mental calmness, composure, and evenness of temper especially in a difficult situation." Equanimity is in essence the most important output that *The Happiness Model* has to offer and directly correlates to inner peace. As we progressively embrace and master the four prior principles, we automatically find ourselves getting calmer and more poised, irrespective of the situation that confronts us. That is, we build equanimity.

Before we delve into this, here's a quick reminder of the four previous principles, which serve as inputs into this fifth and final principle:

1. Spirituality is the goal.
2. Surrender to everything that happens.
3. Perform actions without expectations and with gratitude.
4. Manage your ego.

When you are focused on spiritual growth, accept whatever happens to you as a gift and surrender to it, perform your actions without expectations and with gratitude, and are ego free, equanimity is the result. There is no greater feeling than knowing that whatever life throws your way, you will take it in stride and handle it with poise, mental calmness, and composure. Heaven and hell are states of mind. When we are mentally disturbed, we are in hell. When we have mental peace, we are in heaven. Equanimity is heaven. Equanimity is inner peace.

DEALING WITH THE DUALITIES OF LIFE

Birth-death, victory-defeat, wealth-poverty, wellness-sickness, gain-loss, and so forth are all dualities of life that we are confronted with on a daily basis. We are in a good place when we find ourselves on the easier side of the duality and unhappy when the pendulum swings the other way.

Every one of the dualities we encounter in life is a result of a karmic event—meaning, in one way or another, we caused it. We are human and have emotions, but our ability to control our mind, which in turn controls our behaviors, ensures that we possess the ability to moderate our emotions. We can have emotions without being emotional. Being poised when dealing with life's dualities and not letting ourselves get too high or too low offers a clear path to mental calmness and happiness.

I read a beautiful explanation somewhere about how we differentiate ourselves from the rest of the animal species as a result of our intellect. Nearly all of the animal kingdom operates on the basis of instinct. A tiger can't be taught the virtues of being vegetarian, and a grass-eating cow can't be taught the importance of protein provided by meat. A moth will head toward a flame with no thought of the ramifications of touching it—in this case, death. Humans are the only species in the animal kingdom who have the ability to control their instincts using their intellect. Vedanta goes as far as saying that humans are the only species in the animal kingdom impacted by the law of karma, because we are the only ones who have the ability to control our instincts, exercise our free will, and create karmic credits and debits. Humans are the only ones who can spiritually progress by controlling our instinctual emotions—in other words, we are the only ones who can build equanimity. If that is a vital differentiator between us and the rest of the animal kingdom, one would think it would be a really important skill for us to master.

The following poem by Rudyard Kipling (author of *The Jungle Book*) is called "If" and is one of my all-time favorites. It is essentially a message from Kipling to his son, with a distinct focus on equanimity and its immense value to human character.

If

If you can keep your head when all about you
Are losing theirs and blaming it on you;
If you can trust yourself when all men doubt you,
But make allowance for their doubting too:
If you can wait and not be tired by waiting,
Or being lied about, don't deal in lies,
Or being hated, don't give way to hating,
And yet don't look too good, nor talk too wise;

If you can dream—and not make dreams your master;
If you can think—and not make thoughts your aim,
If you can meet with Triumph and Disaster
And treat those two impostors just the same;
If you can bear to hear the truth you've spoken

Twisted by knaves to make a trap for fools,
Or watch the things you gave your life to, broken,
And stoop and build 'em up with worn-out tools;

If you can make one heap of all your winnings
And risk it on one turn of pitch-and-toss,
And lose, and start again at your beginnings,
And never breathe a word about your loss:
If you can force your heart and nerve and sinew
To serve your turn long after they are gone,
And so hold on when there is nothing in you
Except the Will which says to them: "Hold on!"

If you can talk with crowds and keep your virtue,
Or walk with Kings—nor lose the common touch,
If neither foes nor loving friends can hurt you,
If all men count with you, but none too much:
If you can fill the unforgiving minute
With sixty seconds' worth of distance run,
Yours is the Earth and everything that's in it,
And—which is more—you'll be a Man, my son![13]

One of the poem's stanzas, "If you can meet with Triumph and Disaster and treat those two impostors just the same," is written on the wall of the players' entrance at Wimbledon.

Our attitude as a part of our response is critical when we get hit with something in life that is not optimal. Being poised in tough situations is something we need to work on. Our natural tendency is to let the situation get to us, and then we get bogged down in an ocean of whys. Suman and I were completely submerged in an ocean of whys from the time Zoey was

---

13. Rudyard Kipling, "If," in *Rewards and Fairies* (New York: Doubleday, 1910), 181–84.

diagnosed till well after she passed. Why did our five-year-old have to get cancer? Why did it have to be something so unique that there was no viable cure for it? Most DIPG patients have a period of perceived relief after the first round of radiation therapy; parents refer to this as their "honeymoon period" with their sick kid. Zoey had no honeymoon period, as the tumor continuously grew through the radiation. Why didn't we get that extra time with our little girl? The questions in a situation like this are endless.

I often think about the little kids who were gunned down at Sandy Hook Elementary School in Newtown, Connecticut, in December 2012. With Zoey, we were told that she had an inoperable tumor and knew her time was limited. Imagine the kids who went to school that day and their parents who saw them off, none knowing that it would be their last morning together in this lifetime. Imagine the questions and second-guessing that they had then and probably continue to live with today.

People who put their life savings into the stock market and then watched it evaporate on a tough trading day might have all kinds of questions. Athletes having just lost the finals in their sport may have another set of whys. We encounter challenging situations every single day of our lives, and how we deal with them is an important marker on our happiness curve. The approach I've taken to quell this incessant desire to ask "Why?" is to ask myself "Why not?" I realize this sounds harsh, but sometimes a dose of tough self-love isn't the worst thing. Pediatric cancers are the highest driver of mortality in kids, so why shouldn't it be my Zoey who was impacted by it, causing me to sit up and take notice of this child killer? The world is filled with terrorist attacks, genocide, poverty, hunger, wars, disease, and other terrible phenomena, so when a challenging situation confronts me, what gives me the right to complain? There is a beautiful story about a mother in grief that illustrates this concept.

Buddha and the Grieving Mother

A woman lost her only son, whom she loved dearly, and was overwhelmed with grief. She was overpowered with whys and wanted not only to understand why her son had passed but how she could get him back again. She went to Lord Buddha, fell at his feet, and pleaded with him to bring back her dead son. Lord Buddha, being the compassionate one, felt great pity for the woman and wanted to give her some peace of mind. So he asked her to bring him a handful of mustard seeds from a house where nobody had ever died.

With great hope, the weeping mother went from door to door looking for a handful of mustard seeds. She asked at every house whether anyone in the family had died. Everywhere she went, she received the same sad reply. She was unable to find a single house where nobody had died, so she couldn't get the handful of the mustard seeds that Lord Buddha wanted. The poor woman then went back to Lord Buddha with a heavy heart and told him the results of her search. Lord Buddha explained to the woman how sorrow and death were common to all and that she should not, therefore, be overpowered with grief at the loss of her son. The woman realized the truth of his words and found consolation.

From my own experience, I realize that it is incredibly difficult to internalize this message and build equanimity when you're dealt a deep personal tragedy. The notion of personal tragedy here varies by an individual's perception of what constitutes one. This is where I'd take you back to what we learned from the earlier principles and the law of karma, which says the personal tragedy is a karmic event that is the effect of a cause created by you in this or a prior lifetime. Accept the tragedy with the right attitude and as a blessing from God (Principle 2). Dealing with the tragedy with poise will only make you spiritually stronger and aid in your spiritual development. Every challenging situation is an opportunity for you to continue to grow spiritually (Principle 1).

HANDLING IRRITATION

This is an extremely important element of Principle 5, and I will do my best to discuss it in as practical a fashion as possible. In our stressful lives, we can get irritated over the smallest of things. When the barista at our local Starbucks takes more time than we'd like, it irritates us. The wait times when we call the customer service lines are irritating, and what's worse is the awful music we have to listen to. . . . We really didn't feel like listening to Air Supply the last time we were on hold with our telecom company. The weather, our colleagues, the boss, the government, our family—all end up being natural irritants, probably more so than allergens or bugs. Prior to really delving into Vedanta, I was the most irritable person I knew, so much so that I'd spend as much if not more time being irritated with myself as I was with others. I was perpetually irritated on the home front, and I'd like to think of it as nothing short of divine intervention that my wife stuck it out with me. The constant feeling that I wasn't getting enough time with Zoey (which I discussed in chapter one) would continually gnaw at me and act as an irritant because I didn't know what to do about it. I constantly felt like I was missing something in life and had a sense of emptiness. Not realizing that what I lacked was spiritual consciousness and the associated clarity regarding my primary goal, I would try filling the emptiness with material things, but that only created more irritation. While I was doing well professionally, it wasn't good enough for me. You see the pattern here.

From talking to a number of friends and acquaintances over the years, I know this constant feeling of irritation is not uncommon. Being irritated and reacting to it is a draining feeling and does absolutely nothing to help with spiritual development or inner peace. So why do we let anyone or anything get to us? You may believe that this entire line of thinking is ludicrous and that it is our right as humans to be irritable. The fact that irritability is a core attribute of every one of us is a given, and I don't dispute that in any way. What I'm challenging is the need to let irritability get in the way of happiness and mental peace. What if, when something or someone irritates us, we tell ourselves that the irritation is not permanent and is just going to spoil our mood, and then we just let it go? As humans, we possess the ability to walk away. We have natural instincts for self-preservation, and we need to realize that irritation and the resulting mental disturbance and unhappiness are preventable.

The most pertinent analogy here is that of a turtle. When it feels the onslaught of external pressures, including enemies, the turtle collapses its entire body into its shell. We need to be a turtle when we sense irritants coming our way. Shut down the noise and embrace the quiet within. Don't let the irritant get to you. You will start feeling your natural self-preservation kicking in, and irritation will sweep out of you as fast as it swept in. That is not to say that we can always completely quell the irritation or even a rising feeling of irritation. The point I'm trying to make here is not about ensuring that we never get irritated; I don't think that's humanly possible, and one would have to be extremely advanced spiritually to be at that stage. I'm nowhere near that point, and I can't believe any reader who has picked up this book is there either. My broader point is that as humans, we possess the ability to decide what we want to do to neutralize that irritation when it hits us as an instinctual emotion. We can either feed it or we can use our intellect, see irritation for the useless emotion that it is, and reject it. The choice to let it overwhelm us or to lead the charge in defeating it rests completely in our hands.

Handling irritation with the proper attitude is extremely difficult, and I continue to work on it. I find that this desire to respond to an irritant is the toughest to master with the people you are most comfortable with. I tell myself that this is the case because we tend to take certain people and relationships for granted, but I know that is just an excuse. Give my advice a shot, though, and start walking away, mentally or physically, from situations that irritate you. Be a turtle. You will find that the more you deliberately practice walking away, the more mentally peaceful you will become and the harder it will be for people and situations to irritate you. Irritation in your daily life is the single greatest detractor from inner peace, and denting its ability to affect you will take you a long way toward happiness and mental peace.

EQUANIMITY AT THE PINNACLE OF *THE HAPPINESS MODEL*

Let's look at how Principles 1 through 4 of *The Happiness Model* help us build equanimity. In Principle 1, we saw how we need to embrace the construct that we are spiritual and not physical beings and that spiritual development is our primary goal. This is not about turning away from the material world and shunning all associated desires. The acceptance that we are first and foremost on a spiritual journey allows us to really set the stage of our minds for a transformation of ourselves. Identifying a destination is the first goal of setting out on a journey. The goal in this case is sustained inner peace and happiness. Any and all material objects will only give you temporary relief from life's struggles, because everything the world around us has to offer is temporary by nature and fraught with dependencies. Embracing spirituality as a goal is a-religious. It is about understanding that the only true anchor for inner peace is within you, and if you persevere on that inward journey, you will get to a place where nothing can disturb you, you will be one with yourself, and you will be at peace—in other words, you will be equanimous.

Principles 2, 3, and 4 are about cleansing the mind and removing the impurities that prevent us from realizing and embracing that state of mental quietness. Our minds are in a constant state of movement. In one of the Vedantic texts, the student tells the teacher that the mind is like the wind, and he doesn't think he can control it. I've always appreciated that analogy, because that is exactly how the mind is: all over the place all the time. Expectations, jealousy, hatred, judgment, second-guessing, and other mental activities all take us away from the ability to quiet our minds. Equanimity is impossible to achieve with a mind that is in constant motion.

Principle 2 tells us to surrender to everything that comes our way and to accept it as a blessing. Doing this consistently allows the mind to more effectively manage expectations. When we expect something good to happen, we start building our desires and hopes around it, and when that expectation isn't met, it results in sadness. The goal of the second principle is to treat everything that comes your way in a neutral fashion and accept it for what it is. Doing that consistently helps us to effectively handle the dualities of life and to build equanimity.

While the second principle deals with the act of accepting, Principle 3 deals with performing actions with a clear mind and to the best of our abilities. Performing actions in the best possible manner while managing your expectations of their outcomes allows for cleansing of the mind as well. Imagine the pressure associated with doing something well and then hoping for a desired outcome—that kind of pressure can be draining mentally and physically. Perform the action, and let the outcome be what it may. If the outcome isn't met, try again, and if it's really important to you, don't give up. But each time you perform the action, give it 100 percent and do it with the understanding that you may or may not get your desired outcome and that's OK. Honing this attitude gives us tremendous mental clarity and relief and sets us on the path toward equanimity, because our control points are clear to us.

Finally, Principle 4 is all about working that last and critical vestige of entitlement that arises from the ego. In the thought process of "I did this," the *I* seems to indicate that we had complete control over the process and the outcome. We know that's not true, however. When we embrace the fact that a multitude of other factors all had to align in perfect harmony for our actions to yield the desired outcome, any notion of *I* should be eliminated. When the *I* becomes a nonfactor and we embrace our role in an event as nothing more than a vital contributing element, we start building equanimity. We are comfortable with the knowledge that there are bigger things in play for something to happen exactly as we desired. Knowing the outcome is not in our hands, but that we are nothing more or less than a contributor, creates a huge sense of relief and helps drive out mental turbulence.

ACHIEVING EQUANIMITY

A growing school of thought says that practicing mindfulness by itself can help us achieve and build equanimity. Mindfulness, or being in the present moment, takes a lot of deliberate practice toward slowing down the mind and allowing it to focus on the here and now. When the mind is swirling with a wide variety of simultaneous thoughts and jumping between them, the benefits of mindfulness are impossible to achieve. So how does one work on being mindful? It can be done by embracing the first four principles of *The Happiness Model*, because they are designed to slow the mind down and be accepting of the present, without any judgment or preconceived notions. When we have worked on training the mind to slow down via consistently practicing the principles outlined in this book, we set the stage to be more mindful.

The same is the case with meditation that emphasizes concentration. Meditation is about controlling your mind and bringing it to a point of singular focus, after which the goal is to eliminate that singular focus as well, and revel in the realm of nothingness. The benefits of meditation are negligible for an untrained mind. If a person doesn't have the ability to slow the mind down and quiet it in a sustainable fashion, any positive effects of a meditation session will be lost as soon as the person is done meditating. Meditation is unquestionably an incredible tool for building equanimity, but a lot of effort needs to go into using this tool effectively, and it starts with slowing down the mind.

A key method to achieving equanimity in challenging situations is to tell ourselves, "This too shall pass," along with the reminder that what we are facing is not unique to us and there are others who have had it much worse. In the story about the mother who went to the Buddha for consolation, we saw that in order to be comforted, she needed to gain the perspective that her grief was not unique to her. Really embracing the construct that everything in life is impermanent by nature, including the challenging situation in front of us, is vital. Remember, even if it doesn't immediately look like it, the challenging situation is also a blessing from God and needs to be accepted as such.

Building equanimity, like everything else we have seen in *The Happiness Model*, is a matter of attitude. When something happens in our lives and folks tell us that "God never gives us more than we can handle," we brush it aside as a platitude. But the truth is there is a lot of merit to that statement. We have a very deep reservoir of strength that is purely driven by our attitude. There is nothing we can't overcome and no situation too challenging if we approach it with the right attitude—an attitude that is steadfast in the belief that our psyche is unbreakable and that no matter what comes our way, we can handle it, knowing that it too shall pass.

Equanimity comes from dispassion. Whether in our personal or professional lives, having a high degree of dispassion makes us stronger. A high degree of dispassion can be gained, once again, by taking everything as it comes with no preconceived notions (Principle 2), performing actions without the added stress of expectations (Principle 3), and appreciating that nothing can happen solely because of us (Principle 4). Dispassion allows us to be objective, to appreciate the bigger picture, and to approach solutions with the right attitude. I'm not saying being passionate is a bad thing; in fact, it is imperative that we be passionate about people and everything life has to offer. It is vital to be dispassionate, though, in order to understand that all the things we are passionate about are impermanent as well and can disappear as quickly as they appeared.

Equanimity as a principle is interesting because it is both a vehicle and the desired destination. When we are equanimous, we are peaceful and can live a life absent of sadness. As you've seen in this chapter, it is imperative that equanimity be looked at in tandem with the prior four principles of *The Happiness Model*. Finally, here are some key messages that come to mind when I think about equanimity: appreciate the impermanence of all things in life, embrace change and go with the flow, perform actions and your duty for the joy of doing them and not because you want a certain outcome, and finally, surrender in order to relieve all stress. These messages resonate with me, and I've made them a part of my core belief system. I hope they work for you as well.

CHAPTER 7

PERSONALIZING *THE HAPPINESS MODEL*

Malcolm Gladwell, in his excellent book *Outliers: The Story of Success*, says that we need ten thousand hours of practice at something in order to excel at it. A 2014 Princeton University study qualified it to say that the ten thousand hours needed to encompass "deliberate practice." Practice can be composed of mindless repetitions, whereas deliberate practice is purposeful, systematic, and requires focused attention. If we really want to excel at something and are willing to put more than ten thousand hours of deliberate practice into making it happen, how hard would we be willing to work to give ourselves the most important gift we could ever receive in this lifetime—the gift of inner peace? How much effort would we be willing to put in to attain the ultimate achievement—happiness?

THE HAPPINESS MODEL

The five principles I have laid out in *The Happiness Model* are not merely conceptual. I've worked hard at every one of them and continue to do so, and while I would never claim to have complete inner peace, I can tell you for a fact that embracing these principles has ensured I don't go through life unhappy. I'm increasingly at peace with myself and the world around me, and that feeling of peace continues to build and gain greater depth. I have a lot of work that I need to continue focusing on in order to become a better version of myself, but I feel very confident that I'm on the right journey with the right goals. The bottom line is that these principles have worked for me, so I know they can work for you too!

The reason I wanted to share these principles with you is quite simply because *The Happiness Model* works. With absolute humility I can tell you that my current personality is completely different from what it was before Zoey's passing. As I've mentioned earlier, the voice in my head that I referenced in the first chapter morphed into Zoey's voice after her passing. She has been my guide, and she conveyed to me quite clearly that while her dying was an important karmic reconciliation event for me, it was also intended to give me the opportunity to turn a corner and head in the "right" direction. What that message told me was that this wasn't the first lifetime in which I had been a materialistic, somewhat selfish, self-centered, and irritable person. What it also taught me, though, was that being all those things didn't make me a bad human being, but rather one that is somewhat consistent with the majority of the pack—a person lacking in clarity of purpose in this lifetime and with no well-defined impetus toward any end goal.

The principles outlined in this book are not earth-shattering revelations. While these principles seem intuitive and relatively straightforward at face value, they are not easy to apply. The difficulty is not because there is something inherently challenging about them, but rather because they are based on fundamentally changing our attitude, and that is not easy. It takes a lot of very hard work and very deliberate practice. It takes our changing some of the fundamental instincts that we have honed over the years, instincts that we may qualify as defining us but that in fact cause us nothing more than mental noise and cyclic unhappiness.

When a dog is irritated or uncomfortable, it barks or bites—it can't control the instinct. A moth is attracted to light and heads toward it, even when it will definitely die—it can't control the instinct. As humans, we have free will and are stronger than our instinctual habits, because we possess the ability to accept or reject the instinct. Our ability to control our instinctual habits, like irritation and anger, is what differentiates us from the rest of the animal species and gives us the tag of "most evolved." We can decide if we want to let something irritate us or not. We can decide if we want to remain the way we are or if we want to become better versions of ourselves. One would hope that becoming better humans and being content irrespective of what life throws our way would be the top priority for all of us.

Zoey has been an incredible guide to me over these last five years as I've tried to make these principles a part of my DNA. The feeling of emptiness that I would constantly feel went away when the vacuum got filled with a burning desire to go deeper within myself. Embracing spirituality as my primary goal in life has helped me look at life, work, and the people around me very differently. It has given me the ability to appreciate the important people in my life a whole lot more and walk away from the people who are negative and who try to generate negativity in me. Embracing this goal has also given me a strong sense of purpose and direction, with the destination being within me instead of on the outside.

As you can imagine, we have had a lot of changes in our lives since the passing of Zoey. In 2014, Suman and I decided to move to India, with no concrete plans to return to the US. The old Karthik, who was obsessive professionally, would have balked at an idea like this, because I didn't have a professional network in India, and in this day and age it is impossible to scale any professional heights without a solid network. We moved anyway, and then when it made sense, we decided to move back to the US, just a year later. While we've relocated a fair bit within the US, the prior version of me would have been paranoid about the professional and financial implications of moves like these. The only reason I was able to handle these changes with a markedly different attitude than ever before was because I completely surrendered to what came my way and accepted that whatever happened would be for the best, as long as I gave it my all.

Not being judgmental is a tough behavior that I continue to work on, especially in any corporate environment where some level of political maneuvering is essential and you want to be around people you can trust. Equanimity is something that has now become a very comfortable friend in most cases. The people who do tend to irritate me are ones I'm especially close to, with remnants of expectations from them still lingering on. I continue to work on putting that behind me as well. *The Happiness Model* has helped me find tremendous inner peace in the face of these challenges, and most importantly, in a sustainable manner.

You've heard me mention repeatedly that Zoey is the voice in my head and my guide. As I've embraced *The Happiness Model* in tandem with my inward journey and found greater inner peace, her voice in my head has receded. However, I've developed a method to keep her at the forefront of my consciousness. As I encounter experiences and events in my life, I ask myself if my response to them is in keeping with what Zoey would expect of me. This allows me to make her a part of my everyday life while I also try to diligently follow these principles, which are in keeping with the path she wanted me to go down and the whole reason she directed me toward the Vedanta philosophy.

Our days are filled with challenges, and how we deal with them determines the quality of our lives and our mental states of happiness or sadness. We are constantly faced with forks in the road, where we need to make choices. Virtually every single action, verbal or physical, is based on a personal choice. What if, when you encounter these forks in the road, you focus on the one person you don't want to disappoint and ask yourself if the chosen path would meet her or his approval? Wouldn't knowing that that individual would approve make you a better person and more comfortable about where you're headed? People who feel they are doing the right things are generally happier and lead more fulfilled lives. I find myself constantly asking myself if Zoey would be proud of her dad or disappointed if I did a certain thing, and I've found it to be an invaluable reminder to do more things "right" than not. "Right" in this case is a matter of perspective, with you being the judge. Keeping Zoey at the forefront of my decision-making process has helped me embrace the five principles of *The Happiness Model*, because I feel the intuitive nature of these principles is very much about doing things "right"—with ourselves and the world around us. When we approach ourselves and the world around us with a spiritual attitude as outlined in these principles, we are able to truly appreciate the oneness that exists in this universe, and we can find sustainable inner peace and happiness.

I urge you to deliberately practice each of the five principles in this book and make them your own. Be very conscious of your mind and your thoughts. Rein in your mind if you feel it going astray. Rein in your words if you feel they are not in keeping with your desired goals. Constantly talk to yourself and tell yourself that you can do this. You want to be the best version of yourself. There will be times when you will feel like none of this is worth it and you would much rather "be yourself"—that is, your old self. At those times ask yourself, "Which 'self' am I talking about? The 'self' who is either perpetually or intermittently unhappy, or the 'self' who is mentally at peace and constantly comfortable?" You can give no greater gift to yourself than inner peace and happiness. This life is a journey; I hope you embrace *The Happiness Model* and make that journey an incredibly pleasant one.

ABOUT THE AUTHOR

 Author Karthik Ganesh has been a student of the ancient philosophy of Vedanta since 2013, after he lost his daughter to brain cancer. *The Happiness Model* is based on his own spiritual journey, and he has successfully tested this model for mental peace and happiness in his life. As a seasoned health care executive for over fifteen years, Karthik has published articles in leading industry journals. This is his first foray into writing about his quest for inner peace and how an ancient philosophy still provides a roadmap for happiness in this highly stressful age.

Photo © 2018 At Home Studios

www.ingramcontent.com/pod-product-compliance
Lightning Source LLC
Chambersburg PA
CBHW032044290426
44110CB00012B/952